Network Marketing

How to Promote Events and Growth Your Team

(How to Go From Newbie to Network Marketing Rock Star in Less Than a Year)

Eddie Jordan

Published By **Andrew Zen**

Eddie Jordan

*Network Marketing: How to Promote Events and
Growth Your Team (How to Go From Newbie to
Network Marketing Rock Star in Less Than a Year)*

ISBN   978-1-7780617-7-6

Legal & Disclaimer

The information contained in this book is not designed to replace or take the place of any form of medicine or professional medical advice. The information in this book has been provided for educational & entertainment purposes only.

The information contained in this book has been compiled from sources deemed reliable, and it is accurate to the best of the Author's knowledge; however, the Author cannot guarantee its accuracy and validity and cannot be held liable for any errors or omissions. Changes are periodically made to this book. You must consult your doctor or get professional medical advice before using any of the suggested remedies, techniques, or information in this book.

Table Of Contents

Chapter 1: The Basics Of Network Marketing

If you're considering creating a business in network marketing It is essential to learn the fundamentals. Network marketing, sometimes referred to as multi-level or multi-level marketing, is a type of business strategy that rely on independent distributors in order to market goods or services as well as find new distributors. In this article we'll provide all you need to know to begin your journey into the field of network marketing.

What Is Network Marketing?

The concept of network marketing refers to a type of business model where independent distributors offer products and products directly to consumers, and recruit distributors for their teams. Distributors receive commissions from their own sales, as in addition to sales generated by team members.

How Does Network Marketing Work?

As part of network marketing, distributors usually purchase goods from the business they're associated with, at wholesale rates they then market the products to their customers at retail price. Additionally, they can get commissions for revenue generated by the distributors they hire and future level of distributors.

What are the Benefits of Network Marketing?

One of the biggest advantages of networking marketing is the lower cost for starting. Contrary to conventional businesses that usually require large beginning expenditure, businesses in network marketing are able to be established with small amounts of money. Network marketing also gives an opportunity to work at your home on your own timetable.

Success in Network Marketing

Although network marketing is profitable business opportunities however, it takes determination and hard work for success.

Here are some tips to make sure you are successful with network marketing

Choose the Right Company

In the beginning of an online marketing company It is essential to pick the best business. Find a business with high-quality goods or services you're enthusiastic about. It is also important to look into the benefits of a compensation program and help offered by the firm.

Build Your Network

For success in networking marketing, you'll have to establish a solid group of distributors and customers. Make contact with relatives, friends and acquaintances, to present them your services or products Make sure you keep in touch with them on a regular basis.

Set Goals

The setting of goals is essential for success in networking marketing. Find out what you'd like accomplish, whether that's a specific amount of money or a specific amount of distributors in your team. Then, you'll need to create an action plan for achieving the targets.

Be Consistent

The importance of consistency is for the field of network marketing. It is essential to constantly promote your product or service as well as follow up with potential customers as well as team members and continue to grow your network.

No Get-rich-quick

Network marketing isn't an easy-to-make-money scheme. As with all businesses that requires effort and determination to achieve success.

In this section we reviewed the essentials of networking marketing. We talked about the definition of network marketing and how it operates and what the advantages are of starting a networking marketing company. By knowing this will allow you to begin your own company in the field of network marketing and succeed.

THE BENEFITS OF STARTING A NETWORK MARKETING BUSINESS

The idea of starting a business through a network is a fantastic option to earn a little extra cash and even substitute for the full-time work you do. In this article we'll discuss the benefits of beginning a network marketing company and how it's become a popular option among entrepreneurs.

Low Startup Costs

One of the greatest advantages of starting an online marketing company is the lower cost of starting. Businesses that are traditional usually need a substantial amount of money to start however, network marketing companies can start from just only a couple hundred dollars.

No Inventory

The majority of network marketing firms do not require distributors to hold stocks, so there's no need to put up cash on storing and stocking the products. Instead, distributors usually purchase products as needed that saves in storage costs and shipping expenses.

No Overhead Costs

Another reason to consider network marketing is that there's expenses that aren't overhead for rent, or utility bills, as most distributors are at home. It means that you can begin your own business without having to pay large overhead costs.

Flexible Schedule

One of the major reasons why people start the network marketing industry is because of the flexibility that it gives. Being a distributor, you are able to work at home, and create your own hours. It allows you to fit to meet family obligations as well as other obligations, or even your full-time work.

Work-Life Balance

As you create your own work schedule Network marketing gives you an opportunity for more balanced work-life balance. You'll be able to spend more time with your loved ones, engage in hobbies and other pursuits as well as earn a profit by working on the side.

Unlimited Earning Potential

A further benefit of networking marketing is that it allows you of earning an unlimited amount. Contrary to conventional jobs where the salary you earn is usually restricted, network marketing allows you to make commissions from the sales you make on your own in addition to the revenue generated by your team members.

Personal Growth

Beginning a business in network marketing will also allow you to grow as an individual. As an agent, you'll have to learn skills like sales, marketing, as well as management. These skills will allow you to be more confident, assertive and productive in all aspects in your professional life.

Sales Skills

For success with networking marketing, you'll have to acquire strong sales abilities. That means understanding your product or services, understanding your market segment, and knowing how to convey the advantages of your product for potential buyers.

Leadership Skills

When you're working as a network marketing distributor You'll also have to improve your leadership abilities. This involves recruiting and educating new members of your team in setting and achieving goals and inspiring your team to be successful.

Community

Network marketing can also provide an opportunity to become part of a group of entrepreneurs who are likeminded. This could provide help in the form of motivation, encouragement, as well as opportunities for networking.

Support and Training

The majority of network marketing firms provide support and instruction for their distributors. These include online tools as well as conferences and other events and mentoring from team members.

Networking Opportunities

By establishing your own network marketing company You'll be able to network and meet others who are entrepreneurs. It could result in partnership opportunities, new business ideas and connections.

The idea of starting a network marketing company has many advantages, such as cost-effective startup expenses and flexible scheduling, unlimitable earnings potential, personal development as well as a sense of the community. If you have the right attitude along with the appropriate skills, knowledge, and encouragement and guidance, you will be able to achieve success within this thrilling and lucrative business.

Chapter 2: What Sets Successful Network

Network marketing can be a difficult yet rewarding venture, and it isn't for every person who joins the field. You must be committed, put in the work and a specific combination of abilities and skills to be an effective network marketing professional. In this article we'll explore the factors that distinguishes successful network marketers from others.

A Strong Mindset

One of the most important aspects that distinguish effective network marketers from other is their strong mental outlook. They are able to maintain a positive mindset as well as the determination to achieve success regardless of obstacles and challenges. The most successful network marketers are focused on their targets and consistently take steps in order to reach their goals. They do not let setbacks and defeats deter them. instead make them an opportunity to learn and expand.

Effective Communication Skills

Communication is an essential aspect of networking marketing. The most successful network marketers are skilled communication experts who can establish relationships and communicate with others. They pay attention as they ask questions, then deliver the message effectively and convincingly. They also possess excellent leadership abilities and are able to motivate and inspire the team members.

Consistent Action

The success of network marketing is dependent on constant action and persistence over the course of time. The most successful network marketers have a strong commitment and discipline to achieving daily actions towards their targets. They are organized to set their goals and keep track of their progress on a regular basis. They prioritize their tasks according to their effectiveness and importance by focusing on those with the greatest returns on investment.

Continuous Learning

The field of network marketing changes constantly Network marketers who are successful constantly learning and developing. They are committed to their professional and personal development by participating in events or reading books as well as learning from mentors and business leaders. They are also up-to-date on the most recent trends and technology in the business and modify their strategy to keep up with changing trends.

Resilience and Adaptability

The most successful network marketers are tough and able to adapt to changes. They recognize that setbacks and obstacles are an inevitable part of their business. Moreover, they're able to recover swiftly. They embrace change, and will change their approaches and strategies to meet new circumstances and issues.

In conclusion the success of network marketing isn't an issue of luck or luck, but rather the outcome of a collection of abilities, characteristics and behaviours. Network marketers who succeed have an impressive mindset, strong communications skills, are consistent in their steps, constantly learn as well as being resilient and able to adapt to changing. With these qualities you can easily become successful as a network marketing professional and reach their goals in the exciting and growing market.

THE IMPORTANCE OF SETTING GOALS IN NETWORK MARKETING

It is vital to set goals for every business and individual to achieve success. For network marketing, this is crucial as this is an industry that requires you to be different to achieve success. In this section we'll discuss the reasons the importance of setting goals and how you can achieve goals when it comes to network marketing.

Why Setting Goals Is Important in Network Marketing

The goal setting process helps you remain focussed and focused, as well as they provide you with a vision of where you are heading. When it comes to networking marketing, it is essential to establish a clear vision of what you'd like to achieve and the goals you wish to accomplish. Goals help you realize this vision. The goal setting process also helps you track the progress you make and keep the track of your accomplishments.

How to Set Goals in Network Marketing

For setting goals that are effective in network marketing, you have to adhere to a couple of steps. Make sure that your objectives are precise that are attainable, tangible pertinent, time-bound, and relevant (SMART). These goals must be clearly defined, simple to follow, realistic as well as relevant to the vision you have and include a date.

In the next step, you should break down your goals for the long term into small, achievable objectives that you are able to be able to achieve within a couple of months. It helps keep you engaged and focused while you win smaller wins throughout the process. Write down your goals, and check frequently to ensure you stay focused.

Examples of Goals in Network Marketing

Here are a few ideas of the goals you can establish in network marketing:

Attaining a certain position at your workplace at the close of the year

Growing your sales monthly by a specified number

Enlisting a specific amount of new team members over the coming three months

The development of a certain capability or knowledge that will aid in the growth of your company

Hosting an enumeration of events that are successful in the coming quarter

Tips for Achieving Your Goals

After you've set your goals, it's crucial to set a course of action that will help you achieve these goals. Below are some helpful tips that can help you meet your objectives:

1. Break down your objectives into smaller, more manageable steps

Make a plan or timeline to help you achieve the goals you have set

Keep your eyes on the prize and prioritize your objectives

You must be accountable for your actions and keep track of your performance

Be proud of your accomplishments on your journey

The setting of goals is a crucial part of the success of networking marketing. It keeps you on track to stay motivated and focused on achieving your goal. Through setting SMART objectives and breaking them down into small steps and keeping track of your progress, you are able to succeed in the field of networking marketing.

STRATEGIES FOR BUILDING YOUR NETWORK MARKETING TEAM

The creation of a strong networking marketing group is vital to grow your business and making sure you have lasting success. Building the right team is not something that is easy and takes lots of work and commitment. In this article we'll go over various ways you can utilize to establish a strong and efficient network marketing group.

Focus on Recruiting Quality, Not Quantity

The caliber of the team members you choose to join is far more crucial than amount. When you are building your team you must concentrate on attracting those who align with your goals and who are able to be a hard worker to reach the goals they set for themselves. Team members who are of high quality are more dedicated and eager to see the progress of your company as well as more likely to stay over the long haul.

Provide Support and Training

When you've found a good team members, you need to give them the assistance and education they'll need to achieve their goals. It's about regular communications, training sessions and even coaching. If you invest time and money to your team members they will be able to gain the expertise and experience required to achieve their goals.

Encourage Collaboration and Teamwork

A solid network marketing team can effectively collaborate and work together. Inspire your team members to share their expertise and knowledge with each other and work in tandem in order to reach their objectives. Develop a culture that encourages co-work and collaboration and your team will become more efficient and productive.

Lead By Example

As a leader of a network marketing must be a role model. Your employees are likely to look up to your leadership for direction and motivation and it is essential to establish a great instance for them to follow. That means demonstrating a positive attitude to work, being optimistic and positive, and demonstrating your genuine dedication to the growth of your company.

Recognize and Reward Success

Reward and recognition are crucial motivations for members of your team. If someone in your team has achieved success ensure that you acknowledge their efforts and devotion. This could be as simple as giving them a shout-out in public, or even a little bonus present. When you recognize and reward the achievements of your team, you'll be able to inspire the team members to strive to be more productive and accomplish even greater goals.

Chapter 3: Creating Compelling Content

Today, in the digital world, producing engaging and high-quality content is a must for any network marketing professional. With multiple platforms and channels available it's difficult to figure out where to start. In this chapter, we will discuss some of the most effective ways to create captivating content that connects with the target viewers.

Understanding Your Target Audience

To create engaging material, you must be aware of your intended people. What are their demographics, what are their main issues and what is their motivation? Researching the market and creating buyer personas will assist you in understanding your customers' requirements and interests, which will allow you to develop relevant content for them.

Choosing The Right Medium

There are many ways of making content. These include blogging, social media, content, podcasts, articles as well as many more. Every medium has strengths and flaws, and it's crucial to pick which one is best suited to the audience you're targeting and your message. If, for instance, you're trying to reach a young audience using social media sites such as TikTok as well as Instagram might be more successful over traditional blog content.

Crafting Attention-Grabbing Headlines

The headline of your content is the very first thing your viewers will notice, so it's crucial to create a headline that is captivating and memorable. The headline you choose should be concise and clear and should evoke emotion or curiosity. Utilizing numbers, posing questions as well as a promise of worth are a few effective methods for creating captivating headlines.

Providing Value

One of the primary factors in creating content that's compelling is giving the audience with value. If it's educational, engaging or uplifting your content must provide something that is valuable to people can't obtain anywhere else. Offering value builds confidence and trust to your target audience, and boost the chance of them engaging with your material and, ultimately the business.

Incorporating Visuals

Visuals are a great way to increase the impact of your material, making your content more memorable and engaging. Using high-quality photos, videos information graphics, as well as other types of visuals will help divide your information, making it easier to digest and share. They can also stir feelings and aid in telling the story of your content seem more engaging.

Optimizing for Search Engines

The process of creating great content is only part of the challenge and you need to make sure that the audience you want to reach is able to find the content. SEO or search engine optimization (SEO) is an essential element of content creation that helps increase the visibility of your content and its reach. Learning about keywords study, meta tags and the other SEO best techniques can assist you in optimizing your website's content to be search engine friendly to make it more searchable for the people you want to reach.

Making engaging content is an essential component of a effective network marketing enterprise. When you know your audience as well as selecting the best methods, crafting headlines that are captivating and delivering value, as well as incorporating pictures, and optimizing your content to be indexed by the search engines, you will be able to produce content that connects with your target audience, and produces positive results for your company.

BUILDING RELATIONSHIPS FOR LONG-TERM SUCCESS IN NETWORK MARKETING

One of the main components for success in network marketing is establishing strong connections with individuals. The development of relationships is not just helpful in the growth of the business of your network marketing, however, it can also aid to ensure lasting successful outcomes.

Why Building Relationships Is Important in Network Marketing

The importance of building relationships within network marketing is crucial for a variety of reasons. First, most people prefer to conduct business with those who they like, know and are comfortable with. When you build relationships, it will build trust with your clients and prospects, which makes them more inclined to conduct business with your company. Additionally, it's an entrepreneur-centric industry which means that it's the individuals who propel the company ahead. Establishing relationships can help create a sense of community and individuals who feel a that they are part of the community tend to stick around and expand with the business.

Tips for Building Strong Relationships

It's not an overnight process It requires time and energy. Here are a few tips to build solid relations:

Pay attention and demonstrate genuine interest If you have a chance to meet people, be sure to pay attention to the things they talk about and demonstrate a genuine interest in the lives of those around you. People are grateful when other people are willing to listen to them and demonstrate an genuine interest in their lives.

Maintain contact after having a meeting with someone, be sure to contact the person and keep in contact. Contact them via email or make a phone call to inquire about how they're performing. A regular communication is beneficial in building relationships and keeps your connection going.

Value: Offer benefits to potential and clients by providing them with valuable tips and details. In doing this you are establishing yourself as an authority on your subject and customers are more inclined to be loyal and conduct business with you.

Do not be fake: people can discern insincerity from a mile away. It is essential to be genuine in all interactions. Don't pretend to be something that you aren't.

Long-Term Benefits of Building Relationships

The process of building relationships with network marketers offers many long-term advantages. It is a good start in building a community of partners who will aid in growing your business. When you establish relationships with team members, you will be able to build a sense of community and work together to achieve success. In addition, building relationships can help in building a loyal client base. Customers who feel connected to your business and you are more likely to be loyal customers, and will refer other people to your company. Additionally, establishing good relationships can open the door to opportunities like collaborations or collaborations.

Establishing relationships is an essential aspect of success in networking marketing. If you follow the suggestions and methods described in this chapter you will be able to establish strong relationships with customers and prospects as well as create a sense the community in your company as well as build a devoted customers base. The process of building strong relationships requires patience and time and effort, but the results over time will be worth the effort.

THE IMPORTANCE OF CONSISTENCY IN NETWORK MARKETING

One of the primary elements to be successful in the field of network marketing is consistent. It is about being consistent, committed, and disciplined to your company every single day, despite obstacles or failures. This means being on time with a consistent effort in order to reach your objectives.

The Importance of Consistency

The importance of consistency is that it creates momentum, builds confidence, and builds an established image. When you consistently show up and sharing your story your message, you will be more noticeable and improve your odds of getting new customers and clients. Customers are more likely be able to trust and conduct business with a person who is reliable and trustworthy. It also aids in establishing your image and voice within the minds of your customers and makes it easy to get them to recommend people to you.

The Benefits of Consistency

Consistency can bring a variety benefits for your business of network marketing. It allows you to build solid foundations, build trustworthiness, and bring in individuals who will be a part of your group. In addition, it helps keep the focus, and keep you motivated regardless of the challenges. When you set and achieve consistently tiny goals, it creates an impression of achievement and satisfaction that helps fuel the momentum of your efforts and helps you keep moving forward.

Tips for Staying Consistent

Being consistent with network marketing is a matter of action and mindset. Here are some suggestions to keep you steady:

Establish clear goals Be sure that your goals are precise, quantifiable and doable. Divide them into manageable, smaller actions that you can do each day to make progress towards your goals.

Establish a regular routine every day Create a routine for your day which includes the most important actions that you have to do in order to grow your business. Plan time to prospect in the beginning, contacting people, as well as creating material.

Follow your performance: Monitor the progress you've made by recording the daily and weekly tasks. Recognize your victories and tweak your plan as necessary.

Get support from others: Develop a community of support by establishing connections with similar individuals in your field. Join events, participate in online forums as well as seek out individuals who can provide advice and responsibility.

Examples of Consistency in Network Marketing

There are a lot of success stories of network marketers who had success with consistent efforts and commitment. A prime example can be Eric Worre, who has developed a highly successful business in network marketing and is now an sought-after trainer and speaker in the business. Eric stresses his importance on consistency when it comes to his lessons, and he encourages students to be committed to doing the same thing daily.

Another instance could be Ray Higdon, who started his own network marketing company when he was working full-time. Ray attributes his success to the schedule of prospecting contacting as well as creating content that he continued to do throughout the years.

It is essential to be consistent for a successful business in network marketing. When you remain focused, dedicated and committed to your objectives it is possible to build confidence, gain momentum and be successful over the long term. Follow the advice and suggestions from this chapter to help to stay on track and create your business to bring satisfaction and joy.

DEVELOPING YOUR LEADERSHIP SKILLS IN NETWORK MARKETING

One of the most important elements of successful networking marketing lies in the improvement of leadership abilities. Leaders inspire and direct their team towards the same purpose. Network marketing is a business where the success of your business is directly tied to the performance of your group. This is why it's crucial for you to learn leadership skills in order to build a strong team capable of achieving its objectives.

The Characteristics of a Great Leader

They aren't born, but developed. A few of the traits which define successful leaders are the ability to communicate, motivational and delegation skills and a positive mindset as well as the ability to set objectives. The ability to communicate is essential for networking marketing. You must communicate your messages effectively to the group members. Motivation is also crucial to keep your team motivated and motivated to reach their objectives. Skills for delegation are essential as it is essential to delegate roles and tasks for your team members according to their abilities and strengths.

Developing Leadership Skills

In order to develop your leadership abilities To develop leadership skills, you must put in the time and effort to learn and practicing the essential skills. Participating in seminars, reading books about leadership as well as learning from leaders who have succeeded will help you improve your leadership capabilities. It is also advisable to develop your interpersonal skills through workshops, and one-on-one conversations with the colleagues.

Leading By Example

Great leaders set the tone by leading by. Your actions should reflect the behaviours and conduct you expect from teammates. If you expect the team members of yours to adhere to a strict schedule and punctual, you must also keep your commitment to being punctual. If you would like employees to be productive, then you must work to the max, then you must also be a hard worker. Being an example of leadership can help inspire the team members to follow you.

Empowering Your Team Members

One of the most important responsibilities as a leader in the field of network marketing is inspire the team members. Giving your team members the power to succeed means offering them the tools and support they'll need to achieve their goals. This also includes allowing them to take decisions and responsibility for their tasks. Team members who are empowered tend to be more active and enthusiastic, which can lead to higher performance.

Providing Support and Guidance

As as a leader, you must offer support and direction to the members of your team. It is your responsibility for them to ask questions or address their concerns as well as provide feedback about your work. Also, you should provide them with the opportunity for training and development to assist them in enhancing their knowledge and abilities.

Celebrating Success

Celebration of success is crucial for the field of network marketing. When team members reach their objectives, it is important to acknowledge their accomplishments to remind your team members that their hard labor and effort is valued. Celebrations of achievement can help in building team spirit and inspire the team members to strive more hard.

Chapter 4: The Art Of Persuasion

In the field of network marketing, convincing is an important ability that will help you develop your business and improve the amount of sales you make. Persuasion is the ability to convince people to join your group or to purchase your goods can mean the crucial difference between success and failing. In this article we'll look at how to persuade others within network marketing. We'll also supply the reader with suggestions and tips that will help you be more convincing.

Understanding Persuasion

Persuasion involves convincing a person to do something or to believe in an idea. When it comes to network marketing, persuasion is the process of convincing people to join your group or to purchase your goods. In order to be successful at persuasion is to know who motivates people, and what their wants and needs are. If you understand your target market it is possible to tailor your content to meet their desires and wants.

Building Rapport

The ability to build rapport is an important element of convincing. If you establish trust with someone else it creates the trust and establish a relationship. In order to build rapport with a person it is important to be honest and genuine. Take note of what they've got to say and reply with a manner that shows you can empathize and understand the perspective they have.

Establishing Credibility

Credibility is a crucial aspect of convincing. It is easier for people to believe and respect those they believe to be trustworthy. To build credibility, you should offer testimonials from happy customers or tell your personal success or success story. Knowing the details of your product as well as your industry will help build credibility.

Creating Urgency

The ability to create urgency is an effective method to convince someone to act. In creating an atmosphere of urgency, it is possible to inspire someone to make an important decision or act swiftly. The best way to do this is by making a point of a special offer or highlighting the advantages to taking action today.

Using Social Proof

The concept of social proof revolves around the concept that people are more likely perform a task if they observe other people doing the same thing. When it comes to network marketing, using social proof could be an effective tool to convincing. Social proof can be used to highlight the accomplishments of other members of your team and sharing positive testimonials from happy clients.

Overcoming Objections

There are many objections in network marketing, however, they are able to be overcome through convincing arguments. When someone objects and you are unable to resolve it, be sure to take note of their concerns and then respond in a manner that is able to address their concerns. It is possible to use the data or testimonials you have to respond to the objection and present proof to back up your assertions.

Tips for Persuasion

Here are some helpful tips to make you more persuasive with your network marketing strategies:

You must be confident and excited regarding your company and its products.

Pay attention to your viewers and address their concerns as well as concerns.

Create Credibility by sharing the personal successes or a testimonial from happy customers.

Make use of social proof to show the accomplishments of other members in your group or happy customers.

Make it more urgent through highlighting offers that are limited in time or stressing the advantages from taking action right now.

Resolve any objections with evidence that supports your assertions and responding to questions.

Persuasion is an essential skill when it comes to the field of network marketing. When you understand what drives people, and adjusting your messages according to their desires and requirements and desires, you will be more persuasive and effective when it comes to growing your company. Establishing credibility, building rapport and generating urgency through social proof and getting over opposition are essential elements of convincing. Utilize the strategies and tips provided in this chapter improve your effectiveness as a marketer in the network.

GROWING YOUR NETWORK MARKETING BUSINESS THROUGH REFERRALS

One of the best methods to expand your online marketing company is by leveraging referrals. Referrals are those who have been advised to your company through current customers as well as team members. Referrals are important as they're already keen on your offerings and are more likely be loyal clients and team members. In this article we'll explore how important referrals are and strategies that will help you expand your network marketing company by referring people to you.

The Power of Referrals

The power of referrals is that they are backed by a degree of confidence. It is more likely for people to consider the suggestions of close family and friends rather than advertisements or messages from marketing. The referrals of friends and family also generally have greater conversion rates over other leads.

Strategies for Generating Referrals

Offer Excellent Customer Service One of the best ways to get referrals is by providing exceptional customer service. If customers are satisfied about your service or product They are likely to refer it to their relatives and friends. Be sure that you provide an excellent item or service, and your clients feel appreciated and valued.

Get referrals: Do not be shy to ask your clients or colleagues for recommendations. If they're happy with the product or service you offer They will be pleased to recommend your business to other people. You can make it simple for them to recommend you through an invitation link, or offering them an easy method to promote your company with other people.

Provide incentives to customers: Offering a reward are a fantastic method to motivate referrals. You could consider offering a discount or free item or service for customers who recommend new businesses to your company. It not only helps encourage referrals but will also reward your current clients for loyalty.

Develop Relationships: Developing relationships is the most effective way to generate referrals. Spend the time familiar with your customers as well as team members, and establish relationships with them. If you've established a good rapport with a person is more likely to recommend your services to their family members and friends members.

Make use of social media Use Social Media: Social media is an effective tool to generate referrals. Be sure to be actively engaged on social media, and are posting relevant content that people is likely to find engaging and interesting. Your followers should be encouraged to share the content you have shared with their friends and followers. their friends.

Referrals play a vital role to establishing a successful networking marketing company. They can be a great method of building trust as well as creating new customers. With excellent customer care by asking for recommendations, giving incentives, developing connections and by using social media, you will be able to increase referrals and expand your business through network marketing.

EFFECTIVE COMMUNICATION IN NETWORK MARKETING

Communication is the foundation of any effective networking marketing company. Communication is essential to creating strong connections with prospective clients, team members as well as business allies. Effective communication skills allow network marketers to communicate their messages in a concise compelling, succinct, and concise style. In this section we'll look at the significance of good communication within network marketing, and the best ways to build and enhance the communication abilities of network marketers.

Why Effective Communication Is Important in Network Marketing

Communication is essential in network marketing as it will determine the success or failure of your company. If you lack the ability to communicate effectively are lacking, you will not be able effectively communicate your message to the people you want to reach and, as a result, you could lose potential customers or potential business partner. In addition, poor communication could cause confusion as well as conflicts. It can also lead to losing credibility. This will ultimately affect your company.

Developing Effective Communication Skills

The development of effective communication skills requires time and practice. Here are some suggestions for improving your communication abilities:

Pay attention actively: Active listening is essential to successful communications. It requires paying focus on what another individual is saying and reacting with sensitivity. Also, you should be sure to ask questions and answer any confusion you might have and ensure that you are able to comprehend the message of their words.

Utilizing a simple language straightforward and simple words is essential in the field of network marketing. Your message should be easy to understand and easily accessible to all, no matter what their educational level or background.

Make your message clear: in the world of network marketing, the time you spend is valuable Attention spans of people are limited. So, it is important to be as brief as you can in delivering your message. Make sure you are straight-forward and stay clear of lengthy explanations.

Utilize visual aids including images, videos, or infographics, are efficient communications tools. They are able to help present complex information or ideas with ease and a memorable manner.

Do the practice and practise It's a matter of repetition: the more you work on your skills in communication and improve them, the more successful you'll get. Be sure to interact across different cultural backgrounds, background and ages to sharpen your abilities.

Communication Channels in Network Marketing

There are many channels of communication that are used in the field of network marketing. Each channel has their advantages and drawbacks. The most popular channels are:

Face-to face meetings: Face-to–face meetings are an effective communications tool for networking marketing. They let you establish a relationship that is personal with potential customers or business partners, and present messages in an even more sophisticated and convincing way.

Social media social media sites like Facebook, Instagram, and LinkedIn are fantastic communication channels that network marketing professionals can use. They let you reach an extensive audience rapidly without difficulty and connect with prospective clients and business associates in real-time.

Marketing via email: This can be a powerful method to reach out to the people you want to reach. This allows you to deliver personalized messages to prospective customers or business partners, and measure the success of your communications.

Overcoming Communication Barriers

Effective communication is not easy when it comes to network marketing, particularly in situations where you're communicating with those who come from diverse backgrounds and cultures. Below are some communication challenges, and the best way to get around them:

Language obstacles: Language barriers could cause a lot of communication difficulties. When you're in contact with someone who is speaking a different language make sure you use a an easy to understand languages. Additionally, you can make use of translation software such as Google Translate to help you to communicate.

Barriers to communication: Culture differences are also a problem for communication. Be aware of the cultural practices and beliefs of whom you're interacting with and adapt your message to suit.

Barriers to technical communication: Technological obstacles like low internet connectivity, or hardware issues could make it difficult to communicate effectively. You should ensure you have an internet connection that is reliable as well as a top quality device for avoiding technical issues.

THE BENEFITS OF ATTENDING NETWORK MARKETING EVENTS

Events for network marketing provide the occasion to network with other people who share your interests, gain knowledge from the experts in the field, and get knowledge about the new market for network marketing. Participating in events can help increase your sales, develop your capabilities, and increase your networks. In this article we'll look at the benefits of attending events for network marketing and how they can aid to achieve your goals.

Networking Opportunities

One of the most significant advantages of attending network marketing conferences is the possibility to connect with experts in the industry. The events offer a place where like-minded people can meet and exchange experience. The process of networking can result in valuable connections, referrals, as well as collaborations that could help to increase the success of your company. Through attending events, you will meet prospective clients as well as team members and build connections that will aid you in reaching your goals.

Learn from industry experts

Another reason to attend networking occasions is the chance to gain insight from experts in the field. The events usually feature the keynote speaker and workshops conducted by experienced network marketers that can impart their wisdom as well as their experience. Through these gatherings they can provide valuable insight into the business as well as learn about innovative strategies and methods as well as stay informed about new developments and trends. Also, you can learn from the mistakes and success of your peers, which could assist you to avoid the common mistakes and make your business more successful.

Building Confidence and Motivation

Participating in networking marketing events could aid in building confidence and inspire. In a group of professionals with a love for marketing, you'll find a renewed sense motivation and purpose. Learn from their successes and build confidence in your abilities. These occasions can assist you to create new goals, and then work toward getting them accomplished with renewed energy and passion.

Exposure to New Products and Opportunities

Events for network marketing are also an the perfect opportunity to learn about the latest products and possibilities. The events usually feature new products launches and promotional events as well as attendees get the opportunity to view and test the products. There are also opportunities to find out about business opportunities as well as partnerships that could aid in expanding the scope of your business, and also increase the amount of money you earn.

Creating a Supportive Community

Additionally, attending networking marketing conferences can allow you to establish a strong community. Participants during these occasions can turn into important mentors, advisers, as well as friends that will provide help and support when you are building your business. If you attend events frequently it is possible to build friendships that last for a long time with people from business, and build a an environment of people that can assist you in achieving your goals.

Tips and Tricks

Research the events ahead of time to select the ones that are the most pertinent to your objectives and passions.

Meet other participants prior to the event via websites or social networks to establish relationships prior to the event.

Attend as many classes as possible, and make specific notes so that you can maximize your knowledge and development.

Make time to interact with the participants and speakers during breaks or networking events in order for building relationships and gaining knowledge.

You should consider going to events with your business or team for maximum benefits and to create a sense of belonging within your business.

Network marketing events offer a variety of advantages such as networking opportunities and taking advantage of industry-leading knowledge in increasing confidence and enthusiasm, learning about exciting new opportunities and products in addition to creating a positive community. Through regular attendance at events using the strategies and strategies described in this chapter you will reap the maximum potential benefits and succeed when it comes to your business in the field of network marketing.

Chapter 5: Network Marketing Best Practices

Network marketing is very rewarding and lucrative venture, but it demands careful planning and adherence to some best practices. In this section we'll go over certain of the essential actions to take and the mistakes you should avoid to be successful in the field of network marketing.

Build Genuine Relationships

One of the most crucial aspects of network marketing is building real relationships with your potential customers and clients. That means listening attentively to their requirements, worries as well as their preferences and making adjustments to your marketing strategy in line with. When you concentrate on establishing confidence and relationships and building trust, you will be able to build an enduring foundation for achievement.

Provide Value

In order to succeed in the field of network marketing, you must give worth to your clients. That means providing top-quality goods or services that help solve an actual problem or fulfill an exact need. In providing value and helping customers reach their goals, you'll develop a client base that will be a source of support for your business in the decades to be.

Stay Consistent

The importance of consistency is to be consistent when it comes to network marketing. It means that you show up consistently and consistently in your interactions with customers and prospects offer value and establish your image. When you're consistent in your actions, you will establish a solid presence and establish a reputation within your field and build a loyal fan base.

Spamming

The most common mistake to stay clear of in network marketing is the practice of spamming. The practice involves sending people unwelcome messages, emails or calls with the intention to market your goods or services. This is not only not effective, it could harm your brand and cause people to turn their backs on your company.

Making False Promises

False promises are another typical mistake in network marketing. It involves exaggerating or overstating the advantages of your products or services to gain a customer's trust. This is not only illegal however, it could harm your image and result in losing the trust of your clients.

Concentrating on only recruiting

While recruitment is a crucial aspect of network marketing, it should not be the primary purpose of your marketing efforts. It is more important to concentrate on building real relationships with your clients and bringing an actual benefit to their lives. When you focus on the requirements of your clients and focusing on their needs, you will create a strong customers base that will be a source of support for your company in the long time to be.

Tips and Tricks:

Focus on providing quality and building relationships instead of just selling products.

Make use of social media as well as other channels of digital marketing to reach out to your potential customers and clients.

Be consistent with your work and be present often to interact with your viewers.

Beware of spamming or making false promises as they are likely to damage your brand and cause people to turn away from your company.

Do not solely focus on recruitment; instead, concentrate on building relationships, and providing an actual benefit to your clients.

If you follow these top practices and best practices, you will be able to create an effective and long-lasting networking marketing company. If you focus on delivering real worth to your customers, and developing genuine relationships you'll be able to create a devoted fan base and have a long-term impact. Avoid sending out emails, making untrue promises or focusing on attracting customers, instead concentrate on providing the best value for your money and establishing strong connections with your target audience.

STAYING MOTIVATED IN NETWORK MARKETING

Network marketing is often an extremely challenging venture, and being motivated is vital to the success. Maintaining your enthusiasm is crucial to push toward your goals even when the going gets tough. In this article we'll look at how you can stay focused in network marketing, as well as the significance of motivation to achievement.

The Importance of Motivation in Network Marketing

Motivation is an essential aspect of the achievement of every network marketing professional. In the absence of motivation it's easy to get unmotivated or lose hope in the face of obstacles. An enthusiastic network marketing professional is more likely to invest the work required to create the business that is successful.

Setting Goals

Set goals is an important aspect of keeping yourself motivated when it comes to networking marketing. When you are able to set clear, tangible targets, you have an idea of what you want to achieve as well as helps you keep track of the progress you make. Note down your goals and break them down into smaller tasks which you are able to complete each day or every week. Reward yourself for your successes as you go to help keep you motivated.

Being around positive people

Being around positive people can help you stay inspired in the field of the field of network marketing. The negative influence of people drains your motivation and energy which makes it more difficult to keep your focus in your goal. Look for like-minded friends that are friendly, encouraging and enthusiastic about networking marketing. Join networking events or join online groups where you will be able to connect with fellow network marketers.

Keeping a Positive Attitude

Maintaining a positive outlook is vital to stay engaged in the field of network marketing. The setbacks and difficulties can be expected in the business world, however maintaining an optimistic outlook will aid you to overcome these obstacles. See positive aspects in each circumstance and concentrate on the positive aspects. Develop a habit of gratitude by creating an inventory of the things you're grateful for each day. A positive mindset can help you stay motivated, even during challenging times.

Taking Breaks

Breaks are frequently overlooked, but essential part to stay motivated when it comes to the field of network marketing. Burnout can be a serious risk in the midst of trying hard to create a profitable business. The benefits of taking breaks are that they help get your batteries recharged, decrease stress and avoid exhaustion. Plan breaks throughout the working day, and then take some time off as you're in need. Make sure you take time for yourself is vital to your longevity success.

Learning and Growing

Growing and learning is an essential aspect of maintaining motivation in networking marketing. Keep up-to-date with industry trends as well as attend events for training to improve your skills and tactics. Involving yourself in a mentorship or hiring a professional coach will assist you in taking your abilities up a notch. As you continue to learn and improving, you'll be more confident and driven to accomplish your objectives.

Maintaining motivation in the field of network marketing is vital to your success. Set goals, surrounded by positive people, maintaining your attitude positive as well as taking breaks and improving your skills are a couple of strategies to keep your enthusiasm to a high level. Be aware that building a profitable networking marketing company is a process that requires effort, time and determination, but by focusing on the right attitude and attitude, you will be able to reach your goals and develop your business to be successful.

OVERCOMING FEAR AND DOUBT IN NETWORK MARKETING

The process of starting a new company is a stressful process, and it's normal to be frightened and feel a sense of anxiety and uncertainty as you begin to explore the realm of networking marketing. It's vital not to let these feelings hinder your progress towards your goals. In this section we'll look at some methods to conquer doubt and anxiety within the field of networking marketing.

Recognize Your Fears and Doubts

The first step to overcome anxiety and doubt is to understand what's driving these feelings. Most common anxieties and fears of network marketing are fear of failing, anxiety about being rejected, as well as doubts about the products or business possibility. When you recognize these doubts and fears it is possible to tackle them and then move beyond them.

Focus on The Positive

If you're worried or uncertain, it's simple to be swept by negative ideas. It's essential to keep your focus on the positives of your company and progress. Recognize your accomplishments even when they're not huge as you remember the motivations behind why you began your company at all in the first place.

Take Action

The best way to conquer doubt and fear is to get active. Instead of allowing yourself feel overwhelmed by these thoughts make a plan to move towards success in your company. For instance, you could reach for new clients or following up with current ones, or going to an event to network. By taking action, you can increase the momentum and trust for your business.

Seek Support

The process of starting a new company isn't easy, so it's essential to have a supportive system established. Meet other network marketers on the phone or in person, to share your stories and challenges. It is also possible to collaborate with an instructor or mentor that can offer guidance and keep you focused.

Address Your Doubts

If you're having doubts about the product or business possibility, make sure to discuss these issues. Conduct your own research and inform yourself on the advantages of the product, as well as the compensation program. Contact your top line or representatives from the company to obtain the answers you need to answer your questions. When you address any doubts and concerns, you will be able to take a shrewd decision on the business will be a good fit for your needs.

Practice Self-Care

The process of starting a business may be stressful. It's essential to look after yourself physically as well as mentally. Be sure to get plenty of sleeping in, follow a healthy diet and regularly exercise. Take part in activities that will aid in relaxation and reducing anxiety, like meditation and yoga. When you're looking after yourself, you'll feel better in tackling the challenges in establishing a successful company.

Chapter 6: The Importance Of Mentorship

One of the main elements that will help you succeed when it comes to network marketing is the presence of an experienced mentor. A mentor is somebody that has been successful in their field and will help and guide you through your path towards the success you desire. In this section we'll discuss how important mentorship is in the field of network marketing. We will also discuss how to locate a mentor and what qualities to search for when you are looking for an ideal mentor.

The Benefits of Having a Mentor

A mentor's presence can bring many benefits for those working who work in the field of network marketing. A mentor will provide advice in building an effective business, offer their experiences as well as assist you with whatever obstacles you encounter. In addition, they can motivate you and hold you accountable. you towards achieving your objectives.

Finding a Mentor

There are a variety of ways of finding an instructor in the field of network marketing. Another option is to contact people who are successful in your business or field and request them to become your guide. It is also possible to take part in conferences or events to meet with people within the field, and perhaps locate your mentor. You can also join groups on social media and online communities to meet other professionals working in the field.

What to Look for in a Mentor

In the search for the right mentor, you need to choose an individual who has had an impressive level of success as well as has worked alongside others. You should also find one who is in line with your ideals and goals of your company. In addition, you should locate someone committed to investing energy and time into the success of your business.

The Role of a Mentor

Mentors' role is to help and guide you in your path towards achievement. They will offer advice and provide feedback regarding your strategies for business, aid to set goals and reach them and provide assistance in the face of challenges. They can also relate their experiences as well as provide advice about how they have overcome the difficulties they've faced.

Tips for Building a Successful Mentor-Mentee Relationship

The development of a mentor-mentee partnership is a commitment and effort of both partners. The best ways to create relationships that are successful include having clear goals and expectations communication regularly and in a transparent manner and open to constructive feedback and criticism. It is also crucial to set boundaries, and to respect one another's resources and time.

The presence of a mentor within the field of network marketing can transform your achievement. They will provide direction as well as support and responsibility to assist you in achieving your objectives. In the search for the right mentor, it's essential to select someone who agrees with your goals and values as well as has previous experience in working alongside others. The development of a strong mentor-mentee partnership is a commitment and effort for both, however the rewards are worth the effort.

THE FUTURE OF NETWORK MARKETING: TRENDS AND PREDICTIONS

The field of network marketing has changed significantly in recent years and is likely to change in the near future. The growth of social media as well as the development of new technology and changing consumer tastes are just a few elements that are likely to impact the future of networking marketing. In this article we'll look at some of the latest trends and forecasts regarding the future of this field.

The Rise of Social Media

Social media is a vital tool in networking marketing. It provides the opportunity to exchange information, communicate to potential clients, and create their personal image. Social media sites like Facebook, Instagram, Twitter and LinkedIn offer a great means to connect with an enormous audience fast and efficiently. Social media use is expected to continue growing as time goes on and those who are able to effectively utilize these platforms will gain advantages over rivals.

The Shift to Personalization

Customers today want customized experiences, and network marketing isn't an the exception. Marketers who are able to personalize their marketing campaigns by targeting certain preferences, demographics, or behavior, are better off in the coming years. Personalization requires network marketers to utilize sophisticated data analysis tools to get a better understanding of their targeted audience's preferences as well as behaviors.

The Importance of Transparency and Ethics

Thanks to the popularity of social media and the internet reviews, people are now better aware than they have ever been. They are demanding that companies adhere to a transparent and ethical standard when it comes to their operations. Companies that focus on honesty and transparency will create trust with their customers that will become crucial for the foreseeable future.

The Growth of Mobile

Mobile devices are now an integral component of our lives and it is predicted to keep growing in the coming years. Network marketers that can design user-friendly mobile experiences, like user-friendly mobile websites and apps are better placed to appeal to a larger market.

The future of networking marketing appears bright thanks to the exciting advancements in technology and developments on the horizon. Staying up-to-date on these developments and forecasts Network marketers will be in the forefront and succeed in this rapidly changing field. As the popularity in social media and AI and personalization accessibility, and mobile devices, the possibilities of network marketers communicate with their customers and increase the size of their businesses are endless.

Chapter 7: The Role Of Resilience

Resilience is an essential trait which is crucial to success in the field of network marketing. It is the capacity to overcome difficulties and setbacks and recover from mistakes. In the field of network marketing where failure is prevalent and the path to success may not be instantaneous, it is vital to have resilience. In this section we'll discuss how important resilience is to networking marketing's success and ways to develop the ability to develop this quality.

The Importance of Resilience in Network Marketing

The world of network marketing may be an exciting ride that is not without its fluctuations and ups. Being a marketer in the network there is the possibility of failure, rejection, or defeats. It is crucial to remember that all of these obstacles are element of the process and shouldn't deter you from pursuing your objectives. It is your resilience that allows you to remain focused and motivated in spite of obstacles.

The ability to withstand stress plays an important aspect in building the network marketing company. If you are faced with difficulties and setbacks You make mistakes, and build up your strength. You can deal with difficult situations without difficulty as well as helps you become a more effective manager for your group. If your team members can see your ability to bounce back after mistakes and working toward your objectives They will feel inspired to emulate your efforts.

Developing Resilience in Network Marketing

The ability to be resilient is not something is innate to you but rather a characteristic that is developed as time passes. Here are a few tips to help you build resilience when it comes to network marketing.

Create a positive mindset Positive mindsets are crucial for building resilience. If you are faced with challenges and obstacles, you must concentrate on the positive aspects and avoid dwelling on negative aspects. This can help you keep your focus and motivation high, while focusing on your objectives.

Take lessons from your mistakes: Every setback, failure or loss provides an opportunity to grow and develop. Consider taking the moment to look back at your failures and figure out the things you could do better the next time. This will allow you to prevent making similar mistakes at a later time.

Create a support system: A strong and reliable support system helps you remain determined and resilient. It could be family members and friends or any other marketing professionals who know the difficulties you have to face.

Make Realistic Goals: Creating achievable goals will help you avoid being overwhelmed by the obstacles that you will have to face. Reduce your goals down into small, manageable steps and then celebrate every achievement throughout the process.

Be Careful of Yourself Resilience also means caring for yourself. You must ensure that you're taking enough rest and eating a balanced lifestyle, and taking part in the activities you like. This can help you remain focused and energized.

In conclusion Resilience is the essential element for successful networking marketing. It allows you to remain focus and motivated despite any difficulties you might encounter. Through developing a positive attitude by learning from your errors, building a supportive plan, setting goals that are realistic as well as taking good care of your self and your family, you will build the strength required to attain your goals in the field of network marketing.

THE POWER OF POSITIVE THINKING IN NETWORK MARKETING

In today's competitive market of network marketing, keeping an optimistic mindset is a significant factor to your results. Positive thinking will give you confidence in your ability to confront difficulties and conquer obstacles by keeping you focused and focused on your objectives. This chapter will examine the impact of positive thoughts when it comes to network marketing and how it could impact the success of your business.

The Benefits of Positive Thinking in Network Marketing

Positive thinking has an impact significant in the performance of your network marketing. It boosts your self-confidence and confidence which makes you more successful when it comes to communicating with potential customers and establishing connections. Positive thinking can help to maintain a calm and focused mind, which allows you to be determined and focused on achieving the goals you set for yourself.

The Science Behind Positive Thinking

Positive thinking isn't simply a myth; there are actual studies that confirm its power. Research has shown that people who engage in positive thinking experience less stress levels and better physical health and better wellbeing in the mind. Positivity-based thinking may also boost the ability to think creatively, solve problems and general capacity for resilience.

Strategies for Maintaining a Positive Attitude

A positive mindset even in the face of difficulties may be difficult, however there are a variety of ways to aid. One strategy is to develop a habit of gratitude. Each day, you should look back at the areas of your life you're thankful for, like your health, relationships or the opportunities. This could help you to shift your attention away toward positive thoughts.

Another option is to imagine the success you will achieve. Make time to imagine you achieving your goals, and reaping the rewards associated with success. It can keep you engaged and focused to achieve your goals regardless of difficulties or setbacks.

Strategies for turning negative thoughts to positive ones It's normal to have emotional and negative thoughts It's vital to understand how to control those thoughts to turn these thoughts to positive thoughts. A good way to do this is to change negative thoughts to positive thoughts. In other words instead of being adamant "I can't do this," consider thinking "I will do my best and keep pushing forward." Another approach is to focus on the solution instead of focusing on the problem. Instead of focusing on problems, concentrate on possible solutions as well as ways to conquer these challenges.

How Important it is to Surround Yourself by positive people

A positive, supportive environment friendly people can make an impact on your outlook and achievement. Positive people provide support as well as support and motivation and help you focus in your pursuits and to maintain an optimistic mindset. However negativity can sap your enthusiasm and energy which makes it more difficult to keep your focus and motivation.

In conclusion positive thinking is the most important element to the success of network marketing. If you keep a positive mindset and implementing strategies to manage negative thoughts, you will be able to boost your confidence, remain engaged, and get over difficulties. If you surround your self with positive and encouraging individuals, you will be able to build a positive network to assist you in achieving your objectives.

LEARNING FROM FAILURE: TURNING SETBACKS INTO OPPORTUNITIES IN NETWORK MARKETING

Failure is an inevitable element of life, and it's a part of networking marketing. Each successful network marketer has had to face failure, and made use of it as a step towards the success they have achieved. Making mistakes is a crucial quality to master in the field of network marketing since it helps you to grow and get better at the things you are good at. In this section we'll discuss how important it is to learn from the mistakes you make and how they helps you transform failures into opportunities for networking marketing.

Learn From Failure

The most significant ways to be network marketers is to discover the lessons you learned from your failings. The failure can provide a great opportunity to learn, because it will teach you things you should avoid doing when you are in the future. In the event of a failure networking marketing, it's crucial to set aside time to think about the mistakes you made and think about the things you could have done differently. This will help you avoid repeating the same mistake later on and assist you in learning as a marketer in the network.

Making setbacks opportunities

For Network Marketing, setbacks can be unavoidable. But, it's important to look at setbacks as opportunities instead of as mistakes. The setbacks you experience can offer an opportunity to grow and improve, and could help you to become an effective network marketing professional. If you encounter an obstacle, you should be sure to think about what you learned from your experiences. This will help you pinpoint the areas you must make improvements and will aid you in becoming more effective in the future.

Some examples of successful network marketers who learned from their mistakes

There are numerous examples of network marketers who have succeeded. They took their lessons from failing and applied the experience as a path to achieve success. One of them could be Eric Worre, who is an internationally-known network marketing expert and writer. Worre was a victim of failure in the beginning of his career but utilized it as a learning lesson and eventually be one of the top network marketers on the planet. Another case in point could be Mary Kay Ash, who had several failures prior to launching her own highly successful firm for network marketing called Mary Kay Cosmetics.

How to learn from mistakes in Network Marketing

Failure is a crucial ability to acquire in the field of network marketing. there are a variety of ways to succeed in this process. A good tip is to take your time to look back at your mistakes and determine how you can improve from your mistakes. A second tip is to solicit opinions from other people, since this will help you pinpoint points where you can enhance your performance. It's also crucial to keep your mind focused and see setbacks as opportunities instead of failures.

Chapter 8: How To Identify And Attract Your Ideal

When it comes to network marketing, finding and engaging the most appropriate clients is essential to achieve the success of your network marketing. A perfect customer is one who appreciates your product is aware of the mission you are trying to achieve, and has a desire to establish an ongoing relationship with your company's image. In this section we'll look at strategies to find and acquire your ideal customer for network marketing.

Understanding Your Product

In order to identify the ideal buyer to identify your ideal customer, first you need to understand the value of your product. What are the advantages of your product? And how can it help solve the problem of your intended group of customers? When you understand your product's benefits will allow you to target your marketing efforts at an appropriate audience.

Defining Your Ideal Customer

To determine your ideal client You must identify the person they're. What are their traits such as their interests, preferences, and requirements? It is possible to create a client avatar. This represents a fictionalized version of the ideal client. If you can identify your ideal customer and defining your ideal customer, you can focus your marketing efforts to be more effective.

Conducting Market Research

Market research is an essential stage in finding your ideal customers. It is possible to use surveys or questionnaires as well as focus groups to collect data about your audience. The information you gather will help build a more precise customer profile and help you target your marketing strategies more efficiently.

Utilizing Social Media

Social media can be a great method of identifying and engaging those who are your ideal clients for network marketing. It is possible to use social media sites such as Facebook, Instagram, and Twitter to interact with your audience of choice, publish important content and create connections. Social media allows you to analyze and track the behavior of your customers, which will assist you in adjusting your strategies for marketing.

Creating Valuable Content

The creation of valuable content is essential to securing your most ideal customers for network marketing. Blog posts or podcasts, as well as videos, and posts on social media which provide useful information as well as solve issues that your audience is looking for. With the help of content you create it will help you gain trust and build credibility with your potential customers.

Building Relationships

The importance of building relationships is getting and keeping those who are your ideal customers to network market. It is possible to use emails, Facebook and Twitter along with other methods of communication to keep in contact with your customers, and develop ongoing connections. Through building relationships, you'll be able to build a an enduring customer base who will be a supporter of your business for many long time to the future.

Tips & Tricks:

Focus on quality, not quantity. It's preferring to build a less loyal number of customers who are loyal instead of a bigger number of customers who are disinterested.

Utilize social media channels for listening to your clients and collect feedback. The information you gather will help improve your marketing and product strategies.

Offer exceptional customer service. Answer customer questions or concerns promptly and professionally.

Make use of rewards and incentives to increase customers to stay loyal.

Continuously refine your customer avatar as well as your marketing strategy Based on data and feedback.

Finding and engaging the ideal customers for your network marketing is vital to successful network marketing. Through understanding the product you offer and identifying your ideal client by conducting market research, making use of social media, generating useful content, and creating connections, you will be able to build customers who can support your brand in the long time to be. Be sure to concentrate on the quality of your product, not just quantities, and continue to improve your strategies for marketing by analyzing feedback and information.

THE ETHICS OF NETWORK MARKETING: DOING BUSINESS WITH INTEGRITY

The concept of network marketing offers a company strategy that relies on relationships, confidence, and personal connections. In order to succeed in the field it is essential to adhere to the highest ethical standards and keep an exemplary level of honesty. In this article we'll explore how important ethics are in the field of network marketing and how it impacts your company.

The Importance of Ethical Practices in Network Marketing

The importance of ethical practices is in network marketing as they determine how people view the business. If you are caught engaging in unprofessional actions, they could harm your image and destroy the business. Ethics also help to build trust and establish long-lasting relationship with your customers as well as employees. If you adhere to ethical principles it is possible to bring the right customers to your company and establish a positive impression.

Examples of Ethical Practices in Network Marketing

A few ethical guidelines in network marketing involve being open in your dealings with customers and your team members, avoiding giving false impressions while avoiding ad hoc selling techniques. Honesty and respect for others should be at the center of your relationships with people. It is also important to avoid placing the pressure on others to join your organization or buy your product. Instead, concentrate on building relationships and delivering the best value to customers as well as the team members.

The Consequences of Unethical Practices in Network Marketing

Network marketing that is not ethical may have serious consequences including loss of reputation as well as legal concerns and loss of money. If, for instance, you lie about your product or business idea You could be subject to legal proceedings or be unable to gain your customer's trust as well as team members. Conducting unethical business practices could create negative perceptions in the public and can make it hard to gain new clients or team members.

Tips for Maintaining Ethical Standards in Network Marketing

To ensure ethical conduct when it comes to network marketing, it's essential to keep up-to-date with the rules and regulations that regulate the field. It is also important to seek advice from your top line or a mentor who is experienced working in the field. Also, always remain honest with your clients as well as team members, and refrain from using false statements. Also, you should focus on establishing lasting relationships with your clients as well as team members instead of immediate gains.

In conclusion Integrity and ethics are essential to the effectiveness for network marketing. When you uphold ethical standards will help you create an attractive image, and also attract those who are right for you to your organization. However, engaging in unprofessional methods can lead to grave consequences that include damage to credibility, legal problems as well as financial loss. In order to maintain the highest standards of ethics when it comes to network marketing, be updated on the law and regulations. Get advice from knowledgeable mentors and never forget to build trusting relationships with customers as well as team members.

CELEBRATING YOUR SUCCESSES IN NETWORK MARKETING

Network marketing success does not only mean achieving the stability of your finances or getting notoriety. Also, it is about celebrating the achievements you have made on the road, large or not so big. Recognizing your achievements helps you keep the motivation you need, increase confidence, and improve the happiness you feel. In this section we'll explore the significance of celebrating your achievements when it comes to network marketing. We will also discuss methods to celebrate your successes.

The Importance of Celebrating Your Successes

The importance of celebrating your accomplishments is when it comes to network marketing because it can help you remain focus and committed to your objectives. This can help you develop confidence and create a positive mindset. your self-confidence, which makes it much easier to conquer obstacles and backslides. Recognizing your accomplishments can help motivate and inspire employees and potential clients to reach their targets.

Ways to Celebrate Your Successes

There are numerous ways to celebrate your achievements with networking marketing. Here are some suggestions:

Tell about your accomplishments Your success: Tell your colleagues and potential clients. Tell them the steps you took to get there and the lessons you have learned throughout the process. This will inspire and help others to reach similar goals.

Have a celebration with your team members Enjoy your accomplishments together with team members. It is possible to organize a team lunch or outing in celebration of the accomplishments of your team. It can boost team morale as well as create the feeling of being part of a community.

You deserve a reward: treat yourself to a treat in celebration of your achievement. It can be something as small like dinner in your favorite restaurant, or something larger like a getaway.

Make a board of success You can create a success wall that you display your accomplishments. Include pictures, certificates as well as other items that show your accomplishments. This will serve as a record of your successes as well as help keep you focused.

Make new goals: Rejoice in your accomplishments by setting targets for you. This will help keep your motivation and work towards success.

Celebrating The Success of Others

The joy of celebrating the achievements of others is as crucial as celebrating the successes you have achieved. When you acknowledge the accomplishments of other people, you help create an atmosphere that is positive, which inspires and inspires all those who is around you. Here are some ideas to recognize the achievements of other people:

Honor their accomplishments: Recognize the accomplishments of your team members as well as potential clients. Write them a message of congratulations or do a shout-out via social media. It can boost confidence in them and motivate their determination to achieve more.

Be part of their success Make sure you share the successes and achievements of team members, as well as future prospects with other colleagues. This will help increase their trust and motivate other people to join or help the business.

Enjoy them with you You can celebrate the accomplishments of team members as well as potential customers together. Celebrate with them or give them small presents. It can build a strong relationship, and also build a sense of belonging.

Help them set new objectives: Help the members of your team and potential customers to set objectives to their own goals. This helps them to maintain the momentum they have built and succeed.

Recognizing your accomplishments is a crucial element of networking marketing. It helps you remain inspired, increase confidence, and improve the happiness you feel. Recognizing the achievements of others is important because it helps create a positive atmosphere which inspires and stimulates all who is around you. In celebrating your achievements as well as the achievements of others it is possible to build a vibrant community who support each other's efforts to achieve their goals.

Chapter 9: Network Marketing Also Referred

The field of multi-level advertising (MLM) is a model of business which people sells their products and products directly to customers and receives a percentage of their sales in addition to the earnings of their hired team members. The business model has existed for a long time and has come under the scrutiny of debate and critique However, it has helped many individuals build profitable businesses as well as achieve the financial freedom they desire.

One of the main advantages of using network marketing is its low initial expenses. Contrary to conventional businesses which require an investment of significant amounts in the form of equipment, inventory as well as overhead networks marketing firms generally have a lower cost of starting up and low overhead expenses. This is a desirable choice for people who are looking to establish a company but do not have plenty of money to put into it.

Another advantage of using networking marketing lies in the freedom that it gives. Network marketers are able to be at home and work their own schedules and select their own methods of marketing. They can manage their schedules and commitments, making it a great option for parents who stay at home, retirees as well as other people who wish to make extra money.

One of the most unique features of network marketing is its concentration on building a team. Network marketers don't just sell goods or services to the public however, they also hire and teach team members to be able to accomplish similar things. The result is a culture of support and collaboration in which team members collaborate in order to reach their personal as well as collective goals.

But, it is also the source of controversy and criticism. One of the complaints against networking marketing is the fact that it could appear like a pyramid scheme in which the only method to generate a significant amount of income is through recruiting a significant amount of team members. Although some businesses are accuse of running as scams, a lot of credible network marketing businesses have implemented measures to avoid the possibility of this.

A different criticism of networks marketing is that may be difficult to earn a substantial earnings without having a huge group or an investment in time and energy. Some individuals are in a position to make significant progress with network marketing, others are struggling to make significant revenue.

Even with the disdain that have been made, networking marketing is the most popular choice for those who are looking to create an enterprise of their own and gain the financial freedom they desire. Some successful network marketing businesses comprise Amway, Avon, Mary Kay as well as Herbalife as well as others. These businesses have helped millions of people all over the globe to build profitable businesses and reach their financial goals.

In conclusion the term "network marketing" refers to the business model that lets the individuals market their goods and services direct to the consumer and receive a percentage of their sales as well as the revenue of the team members. This model offers low starting costs along with flexibility, as well as the chance to form an organization and gain financially independent.

Chapter 10: Choosing The Right Company

Selecting the best company for MLM (multi-level marketing) could be an important aspect in your success in this field. With a myriad of businesses to pick from, it's confusing to figure out which one to choose. Here are some suggestions to help you select the best MLM business for your needs.

Study the company thoroughly: Perform thorough research and do your homework about the MLM firm you're thinking of joining. Learn about its past and leadership team, the products or services, compensation plans and reputation within the business. Find information about MLM firms online, via magazines and publications in the industry, as well as through other network marketers.

Review the product or service that are offered: The services or products that are offered by the MLM business should be of high-end popular, well-known, and reasonably priced. It is ideal that they are something you're enthusiastic about and you would want to use. It is important to ensure that the firm offers a clearly defined product range with a emphasis on customer satisfaction.

Review the compensation plans Pay attention to the compensation plan: This is the way you earn money through the MLM firm. Be sure to understand how it operates as well as what the compensation structure is, and the ways you will earn bonuses as well as rewards. Choose a plan that is honest, clear and has a reward to reward your hard work.

Think about the training and support Consider the training and support. The best MLM firm should provide assistance and training to ensure you be successful. Find a firm with resources, such as webinars, training material as well as mentorship programmes. It should also have a solid support systems that is accessible and efficient customer support.

Verify compliance with the law Check for legal compliance: It's important to select an MLM business that operates legally and ethically. Choose a firm that has been registered with appropriate regulators and adheres to a strict code of conduct. Beware of companies who make untrue promises, or engage in misleading or unprofessional methods.

Examine the culture company's culture MLM business is equally important. Choose a firm which values teamwork, collaboration and honesty. An environment that is positive and welcoming could make a huge impact on your performance in your field.

In conclusion picking the most suitable MLM firm could be the most important aspect in your success within the business. Research, analyze the product, compensation plans along with training and support cultural and legal compliance prior to making a choice. By choosing the best company, as well as your commitment and perseverance will help you succeed in the field of network marketing.

Chapter 11: Creating A Business Plan

The process of creating a business plan for networking marketing will allow you to set clear objectives as well as strategies and methods to be successful in the field. Below are the key components that you must add to your business plan for networking marketing.

Executive Summary: The part is intended to provide an outline of your company's network marketing with a objectives, your mission statement and items or services you offer, your potential customers, as well as the financial objectives.

Services and Products: List the items or services that you'll be selling and marketing through your network marketing company. Give details on their distinctive features, benefits and benefits that make them competitive.

Market Analysis: Perform an exhaustive market analysis in order to determine your market's target competitors, market patterns. Make use of this data to develop the profile of your customer and create a strategy for marketing which will be a hit with the people you want to reach.

Compensation Plan The business plan you create should include a thorough compensation strategy that details how you'll earn money with the network marketing company you run. It should also include details about the commission rate, bonuses and other incentives.

Strategies for Sales: The sales plan will outline the way you intend to market and sell to the people you are targeting. It should also include information about your sales channels, marketing methods, and strategies for acquiring customers.

Assistance and Training: If you are network marketers you must be able to provide a solid support and training system set up for your staff. Your business plan must outline the methods you'll use to provide the training and assistance of your team members so that they can succeed.

Financial Plan Financial Plan: Your financial plan must contain forecasts for income, expenses as well as profits. Additionally, it should include information regarding how you'll fund your business in the field of network marketing and also how you will invest profits in order to expand your company.

KPIs and Metrics: Determine the most important measures and KPIs (key indicator of performance) which you'll use to gauge the effectiveness of your company's network marketing. These could be measurements like customers' acquisition, sales volume and team expansion.

Action Plan: Lastly your business plan must contain a comprehensive plan of action that details specific steps you'll follow to reach your objectives. It should also include deadlines, milestones and indicators to monitor the progress.

In conclusion making the business plan of the field of network marketing is a crucial stage to be successful in this field. Through the inclusion of key components like products/services, market analysis, compensation strategy sales strategy, education and support, a financial plan as well as KPIs and metrics, and an action plan that will provide the right path to meet your objectives. If you are committed, diligent and a well-planned strategy put in place, you'll be able to succeed in the field of the field of network marketing.

Chapter 12: Prospecting And Lead Generation

The prospecting process and lead generation are two essential elements for the success of networking marketing. Without an ongoing supply of new customers as well as teammates, your company is likely to struggle to expand and meet your targets. In this article we'll talk about how important prospecting is to lead generation in the network marketing industry along with efficient strategies to find the right customers, and also attracting new team members.

What is the importance of prospecting in the field of network marketing?

Prospecting refers to the act of finding and communicating with potential clients or members of your team who might want to know more about your product or business opportunities. Prospecting is a crucial aspect of network marketing as it allows the expansion of your network and connect with more potential customers who might be interested in the services you provide. If you keep prospecting regularly it is possible to create a team of people that can assist you in achieving the goals you set and increase your company.

Lead generation strategies that work

Here are some lead generation strategies that network marketing:

Social Media: The social media sites like Facebook, Instagram, and Twitter are powerful instruments to generate leads. If you have a robust presence on social media, engaging with your followers by providing relevant information, you will be able to attract new customers and employees who might be attracted by your product or business.

Referrals: Referrals can be great sources of leads for networking marketing. Inspire your customers as well as colleagues to refer acquaintances and relatives to your company as well as offer rewards to those who refer successful customers.

Events: Participating and hosting events like fairs, trade shows, as well as community events is an successful ways of generating leads. Make these occasions an opportunity to present your business and products and meet potential customers as well as employees.

Online Marketing Strategies like email marketing, paid-per-click marketing, as well as search engine optimization are effective to generate leads. If you target your ideal client by using online platforms and attracting potential clients and colleagues who would like to know more about what you provide.

Cold Calling: Despite not being the most well-known strategy but cold-calling can prove effective in generating leads. When you reach out to prospective clients and team members in person it is possible to identify their interests and needs, and offer them valuable information on your services or business opportunities.

In conclusion prospecting and lead generation are the two most important factors in the success of networking marketing. Utilizing effective methods including the use of social media, referrals occasions, online marketing and cold-calling to attract an ongoing stream of potential clients and team members who are intrigued by the services you offer. If you are consistent in your efforts and commitment to building an effective team and attain results in your networking marketing.

Chapter 13: Building Your Network

Establishing your network is an essential component of success in networking marketing. If you don't have a robust community of clients and team members, your company can't grow or reach your objectives. In this article we'll discuss the most the most effective ways to build and growing your network of the field of network marketing.

Make sure you build connections

Establishing relationships is crucial for the field of network marketing. It's crucial to focus on building authentic relations with customers as well as your team members instead of only trying to create the sale. When you establish trust and credibility among your contacts and team members, you will build an enduring customer base as well as your team will be committed.

Provide value

Value is the key in maintaining and building relationships within networks marketing. Make sure you provide important information, tools, as well as support for your customers and your team members. These could be things such as instructional materials, demonstrations of products or one-on-one coaching.

Make use of social media

Social media is an excellent tool to expand networks in network marketing. With a robust social media presence, and connecting with your followers and gaining new team members and customers as well as build connections with existing contacts. Utilize social media sites such as Facebook, Instagram, and Twitter to post useful content, interact to your followers and establish your company's image.

Host and attend the events

Participating in and hosting events could be a great way to expand your network through networking marketing. Make use of events like fairs, trade shows or community events as a chance to present your business and products and meet potential clients as well as team members.

Make to refer

Inviting referrals from your current clients and team members can be a great method to increase the number of people you have within networking marketing. Give incentives to those who make referrals as well as making it simple for customers as well as team members to recommend their relatives and friends to your company.

Personal branding can be used to create a unique image.

Personal branding is an effective way of building networks in network marketing. If you can create a powerful personal brand and branding your self as an authority on your particular field it is possible to build your customers to a loyal base of and colleagues who are attracted by your offerings.

In conclusion the building of your network is crucial for success in networking marketing. Through focusing on establishing relationships, delivering the value of social media, using it to your advantage as well as hosting and attending occasions, encouraging the referral of others by leveraging personal branding it is possible to create an effective and committed community of clients and team members that will help you succeed and develop your company.

Chapter 14: Training And Support

Support and training are the two most important elements of success in networking marketing. While you grow your team, and then expand your company, it's crucial to equip all team members the tools and assistance they require to be successful. In this section we'll discuss the most efficient strategies for educating and assisting your network marketing team.

Offer regular education and training

Training is the key to success when it comes to the field of network marketing. While your team members develop their business, they'll require ongoing support and training in order to conquer obstacles and reach their objectives. Give your team members the opportunity to access training materials as well as webinars and coaching sessions that will help them develop their abilities and grow their business.

Provide coaching and mentorship

Coaching and mentoring the members of your team can be a beneficial in helping you succeed with networking marketing. As as a mentor, you are able to give your team members direction, encouragement as well as accountability, to aid them in achieving the goals they set and to grow their companies. Regular coaching sessions are a great way for your team members in order to remain on the right track and to get closer to their goals.

Create a teamwork culture and cooperation

The development of a teamwork culture and collaboration is vital to the field of network marketing. Your team members should be encouraged to cooperate and encourage the other. Give your team members opportunities to members to interact and work together through team-building activities, like team gatherings mastermind group meetings, mastermind sessions, and online forums.

Rejoice in the your success

Celebration of success is essential when it comes to network marketing. Honor and recognize the accomplishments that your members of the team have achieved regardless of how little. It can boost the morale of your team and inspire your team members to keep in pursuit of their objectives.

Chapter 15: Marketing And Promotion

Promotion and marketing are essential components of networking marketing. In order to build a profitable business it is essential to efficiently advertise and market your goods and services to customers who are interested. In this section we'll look at the most effective methods for marketing and advertising your online marketing company.

Determine your market segment

Determining who your ideal customer is the very first step towards efficient marketing and promotional. Find out who your ideal client is and what their requirements and desires are. This can help you adapt your marketing strategy and develop targeted marketing content that is a hit with the people you target.

Make use of social media

Social media is an effective instrument for promotion and marketing through networking marketing. Utilize social media sites such as

Facebook, Instagram, and Twitter for connecting with potential customers, and also to promote information regarding your services and products. Make engaging content, and make use of hashtags to boost your visibility and reach.

Host events

Events are a good strategy to promote and market your company's network marketing. Hosting product events or webinars as well as workshops to showcase your product and services to prospective customers as well as provide them with an opportunity to gain knowledge about your company. These events can be used to establish relationships with your customers and to generate leads.

Make useful content

Producing valuable content is another successful strategy to use to promote and market your business. Write blog articles or videos that are beneficial to your customers and make you an expert in your field. Utilize content marketing to inform new customers about your goods or services. It will also help buyers make more informed buying decision.

Marketing influencers can be leveraged to increase sales

Influencer marketing is an increasingly popular approach in network marketing. Work with influencers that are popular within your market, and use their influence and reach to advertise your product and services. This will boost your brand's visibility and credibility as well as generate leads for your company.

Use email marketing

The power of email marketing can be a potent instrument for nurturing leads and promote your company's network marketing. Utilize email marketing campaigns to offer benefits to your customers and share details about your services and products as well as promote offers or promotions. Make use of segmentation and personalized messaging to craft targeted messages which resonate with your customers.

Chapter 16: Overcoming Objections And Rejections

When it comes to network marketing, you will often face opposition and even rejection from prospective prospects and customers. Rejections and objections may be challenging to overcome however, they're not impossible to overcome. In this article we'll look at the most effective ways to overcome oppositions and rejections within network marketing.

Recognize the issue

The initial step for overcoming opposition is to be able to comprehend their motivations. Spend time listening to your potential client and comprehend their issues. Make sure you ask questions that clear their doubts and respond to them in a direct manner. Recognizing the issue will allow you effectively respond and create trust with the prospect.

Be compassionate and respond accordingly

Empathy can be a successful strategy for overcoming rejections and objections. Recognize your customer's needs and demonstrate how you can understand their point of view. This can help build trust and foster a favorable relationship.

Offer solutions

Offering solutions is a different method to overcome objections and refusals. Give solutions to the issues of your prospective customers and explain to them how your product service will meet their requirements. Offer cases and examples to show the worth of your product or service.

Resolve common issues proactively

Engaging in proactive responses to common objections is an efficient strategy for getting past rejections and obstacles. Prepare for common objections and answers in advance. This can help you react quickly and efficiently and increase confidence in your potential client.

Make use of testimonials and social proof

Social proof and testimonials can be a powerful strategy to getting past opposition and rejection. Use testimonials and case studies of satisfied clients to prove the worth of your service or product. Make use of social proof, like customer reviews or ratings to increase credibility and confidence in your prospective customers.

Follow up

Follow-up is an essential approach to overcoming objections or rejections. Keep in touch with your prospects when you have addressed their concerns, to determine what they might have further issues or questions. Keep in contact and offer regular support to help build relationships and trust with your prospects.

In conclusion defeating oppositions and rejects is an essential skill for network marketing. When you understand the reason for an objection and responding in a compassionate manner by offering a solution, responding to the common pitfalls, utilizing testimonials, social proof and other evidence and then taking action with a positive response, you will be able to overcome the objections and rejects, and create the foundation for a profitable network marketing business.

Chapter 17: Duplication And Scaling

The duplication and scaling of your business are essential factors in the success of network marketing. In this section we'll look at how important it is to have duplication and scaling, and offer strategies to getting both of them within your network marketing company.

Duplication

The process of duplication involves instructing others on how to perform the same thing you are doing. In the field of network marketing, duplicate is crucial to building an effective team as well as expanding the business you run. In order to achieve duplication it is necessary to create an effective system that is easy to implement and replicable. Below are some methods for getting duplication

Create a step-by-step method Make a clear steps-by-step method that you and your team will use to develop their company. It should be simple to comprehend and replicate and must include the most essential components of network marketing including prospecting as well as lead generation, follow-up and sales.

Training and Support: Give training and support to your staff to aid them in learning how to use the system, and acquire the necessary skills to achieve success. It could be through regular webcasts, training or coaching sessions, as well as mentoring.

Leap by example: lead by example, and then demonstrate the process yourself. Let your team know how you accomplish what you are doing and become an example of success in your own business.

Scaling

The process of scaling is developing your business, and expanding the scope of your services. When it comes to networking marketing, it is crucial for bringing in greater numbers of people in sales growth, increasing revenue, as well as building a larger team. Here are some methods for reaching a higher level of scaling

Make use of technology to streamline and automate your processes for business. This can include the use of social media, email marketing as well as automated follow-up technology.

Concentrate on activities that have the highest impact Concentrate on activities with high impact which produce the greatest positive results for your company. It could be lead generation, prospecting, as well as follow-up.

Reach out to more people: Increase your possibilities by investigating the new demographics and markets. You might consider expanding your product range or looking to expand your customer base.

Establish a leadership team Create a team of leaders that can help you run and expand your company. It could involve promoting the individuals who are top of the line within your organization as well as recruiting new managers to assist you in your efforts to increase your growth.

Chapter 18: Managing Your Finances

The management of your finances is a crucial aspect of operating a successful marketing network. In this article we'll discuss ways to manage your financials and maintaining the security of your company's finances.

Set a Budget

The initial step to manage your financial situation is setting an appropriate budget. Find out your expenses and income and develop a budget which defines your expenses each month. Be sure to list the costs of purchasing products as well as marketing and advertising and other expenditures that are related to the running of your company.

Track Your Expenses

It's crucial to monitor the expenses on a regular basis to ensure you're staying within the budget you have set. Utilize a spreadsheet, or an software for accounting to monitor your earnings and expenditures in addition to keep your financial accounts in check to make sure that everything is in order.

Separate Personal and Business Finances

The most frequent error made by network marketers is mixing their personal and business financial accounts. It's crucial to keep these two financial accounts separate in order to avoid confusion, and to ensure that your accounting is accurate. Create a separate bank account and credit card to your business, and make use of them only for your business's costs.

Build an Emergency Fund

The creation of an emergency fund is vital to ensure the security of your company. Make sure to set aside a part of your monthly income to create an emergency fund which can be used to cover any unexpected costs or decrease in revenue.

Invest in Your Business

Making investments in your business is essential for the long-term growth of your business. Set aside a percentage of your monthly income to fund equipment, training as well as resources to aid in the growth of your company. It can include investing in advertising and marketing or attending conferences and other events and employing a mentor or coach.

Plan for Taxes

Taxes are a major expense for network marketers therefore it is important to prepare for these expenses. Make sure to set aside a percentage of your monthly income for taxes. Also, make sure you keep precise records of all expenses in order so that you can maximize deductions.

Chapter 19: Time Management And Productivity

The management of time and the productivity are the most important factors to performance of any network marketing company. In this article we'll look at some ways to manage your time efficiently and boosting your efficiency.

Set Clear Goals

First step for efficient time management is setting specific objectives. Establish your short-term and long-term objectives and then break them into manageable, smaller projects. Set priorities for your work and concentrate on the top priorities first.

Create a Schedule

The creation of a calendar is crucial for efficient time control. Schedule specific time slots to perform tasks like following-up, prospecting for training, as well as other administrative duties. Utilize a planner or a digital calendar to keep well-organized and ensure you're making the most of your time.

Eliminate Time Wasters

Find any distractions in your life and remove the sources of distraction. These could be related to emails, social media and other distracting activities that hinder your productive time. You should set specific times to check emails or social media be sure to not check these outside of the time frames.

Delegate Tasks

It is helpful to delegate work and get more time to do other crucial work. Consider tasks that are assigned to other people like administrative duties or calls to follow up, and look into hiring an assistant, or outsource these tasks to freelancers.

Use Time-Saving Tools

There are a variety of tools which can save you time as well as increase efficiency. Utilize tools like automated software as well as social media scheduling software and email templates to simplify your work and get the most out of your time.

Take Breaks

It is crucial to take breaks for maintaining your work efficiency and to avoid burning out. Make sure to take breaks regularly throughout your working day to refresh and focus your energies. It could be an exercise, sitting in a meditation, or simply taking a break from your desk for a short period of time.

Prioritize Self-Care

Last but not least, you must prioritize your self-care routine for maintaining your work efficiency and overall energy. Take time to exercising, eating healthy, as well as other activities to will keep you on track and invigorated.

Chapter 20: Maintaining Motivation And Persistence

Motivation and perseverance are vital to success when it comes to network marketing. In this section we'll look at some methods to remain determined and focused when faced with difficulties and setbacks.

Set Realistic Expectations

One of the primary reason why people aren't motivated for network marketing is the fact that they have false expectations. Recognize that running an effective business requires patience and time There will have ups and downs along the journey. Make realistic targets and concentrate in achieving these targets.

Find Your Why

The process of determining your "why" and the motivation behind why you're building your own network marketing company is a potent incentive. Consider taking time to reflect on your passions, values and objectives, then link them with your company. A strong sense of the purpose of your business can keep you engaged even when the going gets challenging.

Celebrate Small Wins

Small wins are a great way to aid in staying focused and work towards the goals you have set. Be sure to recognize and praise even the most insignificant achievements like getting in touch with a particular amount of potential customers or closing the first transaction. Recognizing these achievements can aid in staying motivated as well as help you to keep moving towards bigger goals.

You can surround yourself with supportive people

Being surrounded by people who are supportive could make a huge improvement in drive and determination. Join with network marketers with similar desires and goals, as well as find coaches and mentors who will provide advice and help. Be part of a supportive group can allow you to stay engaged and overcome difficulties.

Embrace Failure as a Learning Opportunity

As in all businesses, failing will happen. Instead of not letting your failures discourage you, make it an opportunity to learn. Review what went wrong and how you could do it better next time around, and then use the knowledge you learnt to implement improvements in your company.

Take Action Even When You Don't Feel Like It

One key to sustaining determination and motivation is taking steps even when you're not feeling motivated. There will be moments when you're feeling discouraged or demotivated However, doing something - even little actions can allow you to overcome that negative feelings and gain momentum toward the goals you have set.

In conclusion, retaining motivation and persistence are essential to successful networking marketing. Through setting realistic goals by identifying your motivation and celebrating the small victories and surrounding yourself with positive members, accepting defeat as a chance to learn from it as well as taking action when you're not feeling at the moment, you'll be able to remain motivated and persevering when faced with difficulties and failures.

Chapter 21: Leadership And Team Building

Building teams and leadership are crucial to successful networking marketing. In this article we'll discuss methods for gaining solid leadership abilities and for building an effective team.

Lead by Example

One of the key characteristics of a great leader is the ability to model. Show the behaviors and behavior that you would like employees to follow. Teach them how to make prospect as well as follow up and then close the sale effectively. In your role as a leader and demonstrating the knowledge and attitudes that are required to succeed in network marketing.

Develop Strong Communication Skills

Effective communication is the key in building a strong team. As an executive, you must to convey your goals, visions, and expectations in a clear manner to your teammates.

Additionally, you must be an effective listener, adept at recognizing the requirements and issues of the team members and communicate effectively. Make sure you are developing your skills in communication through practice through feedback, training, and practice.

Empower Your Team Members

In order to empower your team members, you must offering them the necessary tools, resources and guidance they require to succeed. Help them take charge of their own company create goals, establish objectives and then take steps toward achieving these goals. Offer training, coaching and guidance to grow their capabilities and boost confidence. When you empower your employees, you help create an environment of achievement and encourage long-term growth.

Foster a Positive Culture

A positive and supportive culture is crucial to build an effective team. Recognize and praise good performance as well as create a sense cohesion and community within the team. Help team members support one another, and to work to achieve the same targets. Through fostering a positive environment and a positive team, you can create one which is enthusiastic, involved and committed to the success of their company.

Provide Ongoing Support and Training

Continuous support and ongoing training is vital to ensure the continued growth and development of your staff. Offer regular instruction on new strategies for sales, new products and other skills which are pertinent to the success of your team. Provide support and direction to members of your team who are having difficulty, and guide them to create strategies for dealing with difficulties. Through continuous support and education to your team, you can help members develop and become entrepreneurs.

In conclusion the leadership skills and team-building are crucial abilities for success in network marketing. Through leading with a clear example, learning strong communication abilities, supporting the team members in your organization, creating an environment that is positive, as well as by providing continuous support and education to build a team that's motivated by, engaged and committed to a long-term plan of growth.

Chapter 22: Managing Your Mindset And Emotions

The ability to control your mind and emotions is essential to the success of the field of network marketing. In this section we'll discuss methods to help you develop an optimistic mindset as well as controlling your emotions successfully.

Focus on the Positive

Positive thinking is crucial to succeed when it comes to networking marketing. Instead of focusing in the negative, you should focus on the positives of your venture. Recognize your accomplishments however small they might be. When you concentrate on the positives and focusing on the positive, you will remain motivated and motivated even when you are faced by setbacks and challenges.

Develop Resilience

Resilience means the capacity to bounce back after defeats and difficulties. It's a vital quality for success in network marketing, a field

148

where it is not uncommon to experience failures and rejection. In order to build resilience, concentrate on cultivating a mindset of growth that sees the challenges as an opportunity to improve and grow. Take your lessons learned from mistakes and apply them to enhance your strategies and skills.

Practice Self-Care

Network marketing is an extremely stressful and demanding business. It's important to ensure your emotional and physical health. Pause when you're in need of to, regularly exercise as well as eat a nutritious diet and take adequate sleeping. Try relaxation methods such as deep breathing or meditation to reduce anxiety and stress.

Develop Emotional Intelligence

The ability to manage and recognize the emotions of your own, in addition to the emotional state of other people. For networking marketing, it's crucial to empathize and connect with potential clients and colleagues. The development of emotional intelligence will aid in building stronger connections and improve your communication.

Be Positive and surround yourself with positive influences

A positive environment helps you stay focused and stay positive. Join networks with successful marketers, study books and reviews on personal development as well as success in business, and find experts who can give assistance and guidance.

In conclusion managing your thoughts and emotional state is vital to the success of network marketing. If you focus on the positive aspects, gaining self-care habits and enhancing your emotional intelligence and surrounded by positive influencers, you can create the mindset and mental ability to succeed in the field of network marketing.

Chapter 23: Achieving Success And Financial Freedom

The pursuit of financial freedom and success is the main goal for the majority of network marketers. In this article we'll discuss important strategies to achieve prosperity and financial independence within the field of network marketing.

Set Clear Goals

The setting of clear, specific goals is vital to achieve successful networking marketing. Your objectives should be realistic as well as measurable and time-bound. Note down your goals and revisit them frequently to keep you engaged and on track.

Develop a Solid Strategy

For success when it comes to networking marketing, you must have an effective plan. It should contain an organized plan for the prospecting process and lead generation as well as developing your network, advertising your business and managing your financials.

You should constantly review and tweak the strategy you have in place to ensure your strategy is efficient and aligned with your business goals.

Take Consistent Action

Continuous action is essential to the success of networking marketing. Make sure you set aside time every day or every week to work to improve your business and adhere to the schedule you have set. Concentrate on activities with high impact that assist you in achieving your goals. This includes making contact with prospects and following up on leads.

Embrace Continuous Learning

When it comes to the world of network marketing, it's important to constantly learn and expanding. Participate in training sessions, read publications and other articles Find experts and mentors who will assist you in improving your abilities and understanding. Learning continuously can keep you engaged and keep up with the constantly changing landscape of networking marketing.

Provide Value and Serve Others

In order to succeed when it comes to network marketing, it's essential to add value and help the needs of others. Be focused on satisfying the requirements and addressing the issues of both your team and prospective members. In delivering value and serving other people, you will create trust, credibility as well as a loyal fan base that will allow you to attain lasting success.

In conclusion getting to the top and achieving success and financial independence in the field of network marketing means setting specific objectives, creating a strong strategy, making sure you are taking action consistently as well as embracing ongoing learning offering value, and helping other people. If you follow these techniques, you can create a your own successful business in network marketing which gives you flexibility, time as well as the financial means to realize your goals and live according to your preferences.

Chapter 24: Understanding Network Marketing

1.1 Definition and Overview

This chapter will give you the complete overview of network marketing often referred to as multi-level marketing (MLM) in this section. The foundation of your business's success is a matter of understanding the basic concepts and theories that make up network marketing.

The sale of products and services by a group of agents or distributors who are independent is at the heart of the business model. Network marketing companies are based on a community of companies that advertise and market their goods directly to consumers in contrast to traditional channels for marketing, which rely on brick-and-mortar stores and marketplaces.

The principle underlying networking marketing is the idea that distribution companies be paid for their own earnings and the sales of their team. members. Distributors are enticed through this distinct pay scheme to assist others in starting their own companies in helping recruit employees and attracting them.

Network marketing firms offer an array of products and services. These include nutrition supplements to improve health and wellness products, skincare and cosmetics such as home products along with financial services and much more. The companies often emphasize the value and high-quality of their products and distributors are essential in the promotion of these products by offering suggestions as well as demonstrations.

The attraction of network marketing is in its capability to supply individuals from every walk of life with an affordable risk business venture. There is no upfront investment or requirement for the creation of products or control of inventory, and the flexibility to work whenever and however they like the network allows people to create their own companies. The entire network has to work in tandem in order for the network marketing system to be effective, creating a co-operative and friendly community.

As time passes, the concept of networking marketing has shifted and has become an acceptable business practice. Numerous successful businesspeople as well as influential people in the field have been a part of the world of network marketing despite the mistrust and myths which persist. The network marketing industry is an effective way towards financial freedom along with personal development and the possibility of having an impact on the lives of others.

The many aspects of marketing through networks are covered in this book. It will cover winning strategies and effective sales strategies and team-building, using technologies, overcoming obstacles as well as ethical behaviour. You'll be in your ability to manage the company to make the most of opportunities and achieve your objectives if you've got an in-depth understanding of the field of network marketing.

Let's look at the growth of network marketing more depth now that we have the clearest definition and outline of the process.

1.2 Evolution of Network Marketing

Knowing the growth of network marketing is vital to be aware of its present state and the potential for future developments. Network marketing is a storied background that spans many years. Network marketing has undergone significant changes over time as a result shifts in the dynamics of markets technological advancements, as well as shifts in the behavior of consumers.

The beginnings of network marketing could be traced to the latter half of the 20th century as businesses began to look at alternative distribution methods. Direct selling, which was the process of were able to sell goods directly to clients in non-traditional retail locations was developed during the 1950s and

1940s. Businesses were able to reach clients faster due of this direct selling method as well as gave individuals the opportunity to earn profits through sales that were independent.

The modern concept of network marketing that we are familiar with today took shape during the 1970s. The concept of multi-level marketing (MLM) gained more recognition in the course of this time. The MLM industry developed a compensation system that compensated distributors for their own earnings as well as profits made by those within their downline. The distinctive network marketing business model was based around a system that provided an incentive to the development of teams and for recruiting.

Network marketing saw a huge increase in popularity during the late 1980s and early 1990s that was fueled through the growth of large firms in the field. The companies, who often were focusing on wellness and health merchandise, drew the attention of entrepreneurs who wanted to be successful and were searching for a completely different work.

Success stories from the people who utilized network marketing to be financially self-sufficient helped to validate the model of business and draw more people to the industry.

Network marketing began a new stage in the 1990s, and into the 2000s following the advent to the world wide web. Distributors now have the chance to promote their brand increase their network, and communicate with a wider crowd thanks to internet-based instruments and networks. Furthermore, the internet has provided better methods of communicating, education and help, providing distributors with essential tools and data.

Network marketing has expanded over the last few years as a response to the changing organizational conditions. In order to expand their reach and enhance the customer experience, companies have been utilizing methods of digital marketing, such as social media platforms and E-commerce solutions.Automation as well as technological advances simplify operations, improved the effectiveness of distributors, as well as given them powerful management abilities.

Network marketing is an incredibly successful and growing industry that is international today. People are now considering that it is a valid career choice because it offers people the opportunity to try the entrepreneurial spirit, be financially secure and live a more flexible life. It is constantly creating new and innovative ideas and adapting to market shifts by offering new products and services.

It's essential to know about the development of network marketing and the lessons learned along the way as you travel through the field. It is possible to learn about the fundamental ideas of the field along with the most effective practices and future possibilities when you study its past. The growth of network marketing shows its persistence and capability to change, which is why it's an exciting and exciting field that is a dream for entrepreneurs who want to be successful.

The benefits as well as the drawbacks to networking marketing in the chapters which are to follow.

1.3 Benefits and Challenges of Network Marketing

Many of the advantages that network marketing offers have attracted thousands of individuals across the globe to the business model. But, it's not without some challenges as with every other business venture. The following article will explore the pros and drawbacks of networking marketing in this article, providing an objective view as you embark on your journey.

Benefits of Network Marketing:

Flexible and free Flexibility and Freedom: Network marketing offers an opportunity to be a self-employed professional and work at your own pace. It is possible to set your own schedule and work from anywhere and build a company which meets your personal and financial goals. You could design a balance between work and life that is in your best interests.

The low cost of starting a business Network marketing is less of a barrier to entry as compared to traditional methods of business. The purchase of a starter kit or product inventory can be the sole major upfront cost. No matter what your financial standing it is easy to get involved in network marketing thanks to its affordable cost.

Help and training: Trustworthy companies that operate through networks offer their distributors with comprehensive training and ongoing assistance. They can benefit by the experience and expertise from senior executives in the corporate world that are committed to your success. Most often, the top salesperson hires fresh salespeople for the company. Then, you could have the possibility of receiving guidance from the recruiter in return. Because it helps the recruiter, they can assist you in learning how to do the process and help you increase sales. An alliance that is beneficial to both sides is formed by boosting your sales. It is possible to grow your business using the mentoring and training options which are available.

Utilizing personal Networks Utilizing Personal Networks: Network marketing utilizes the power of your personal networks. It is possible to network with people around the world and expand your circle and create partnerships.You can access an array of prospective clients as well as team members via excellent networking. It opens doors to growth and even financial potential.

Possibility of passive income: One of the major advantages of networking marketing is the potential for the possibility of passive income. There is a chance to generate residual earnings from sales generated by your group as you build the team as well as leaders in your business. You can earn cash even when you're active in direct selling due the passive income stream.

Challenges of Network Marketing:

In the face of doubt and rejection, network marketing is often a source of doubt or miscommunications that can lead to rejection from prospective clients or even team members. A strong sense of resiliency, a solid communication skills and an ardent commitment to spreading information on the benefits of network marketing as a model for business is essential to overcome the obstacles.

Initial effort and commitment to time Beginning your own network marketing business requires commitment, persistence, and a steady, consistent work. Finding clients, prospecting for them and establishing an organization can require considerable time and energy initially. The benefits of a successful business may not be realized for a long time and the success of a business is directly dependent on the level of effort put into.

Leadership and Building a Team The building of teams is an essential aspect of marketing via networks, however it can be a challenge. Leadership, support as well as training are crucial to the formation of a successful team. Making sure you balance your business's performance with that of the team members could be challenging.

Market saturation and competition: Because of increase in competition within certain networks marketing areas, it could be more challenging to distinguish yourself and gain customers and team members. In order to be competitive you must be different from others and offer something that no one could else, and continually change to market trends.

maintaining personal relationships Network marketing often involves making contact with relatives, friends or acquaintances in order to provide details about your products or business venture. To maintain strong connections, you must have care, respect, and clear communication, while also balancing your personal and professional relationships.

There will be disappointments from the people you attempt to attract for your company:

They'll try to change your mind. In fact, they'll try to influence your opinion. Certain people do not desire you to achieve success It's true, you'll find out. They'll say things designed to derail you and make you quit. You've probably been told, "I knew a guy who joined one of these deals and it didn't work out." Be aware that, despite your exuberance, there are people who still not quite ready. Keep in touch with these people. Regularly make contact with them to find out how things are going and to determine whether they're keen to know more.

Employees from other companies will be able to approach the leaders of your team: They might lose some members due in the process of hiring. This happens to everybody. The fact that you don't "own" anyone in your business is key. The company is in collaboration. There are some who will search at alternative options. Don't let this cause a rift in your relationship. The two of you could work together once again in the near future. However, if you're working with someone other than you, be sure to congratulate them for your accomplishment. There may be opportunities for collaboration again in the near future.

Chapter 25: Setting Yourself Up For Success

2.1 Mindset and Attitude

The mindset and the attitude of a person are crucial to achieving success

with network marketing, or any other enterprise. In order to overcome challenges, maintain the motivation to achieve your goals, it's vital to develop the correct attitude and mindset. This chapter will examine the significance of thoughts and attitude when it comes to network marketing. It will also provide actions you can follow to ensure your successful results.

Your thoughts, opinions and beliefs that influence your perception of you and the world around your are known as your attitude. It influences your approach to challenges, handle failures and take advantage of opportunities. It is vital to have a growth mindset to network marketing as it helps you accept taking risks, learn from your mistakes and remain positive even in the face of failure.

Below are a few key aspects of a successful mindset networking marketing:

Believe in yourself and your business Network marketing professionals should have faith unshakeable in themselves as well as their company. Know that achieving success is achievable and feasible. Be confident in the products or services you're selling and the advantages they bring to the customers. The conviction you have will not just affect your behaviour but it will inspire confidence in your customers.

adopting a learning Mindset Network marketing is an area that's constantly changing so being ready to new knowledge. Find opportunities to further your knowledge by participating in corporate training programs, business conferences or publications, podcasts or through mentoring. Always be open to new concepts as well as eager to adapt and enhance your practices.

Accepting failure and learning from setbacks: Setbacks as well as failings are part of networking marketing just similar to any other business. It is crucial to adopt an outlook that regards the setbacks as opportunities to develop and improvement. Instead of focusing on the mistakes review them carefully and draw lessons using the lessons to enhance your strategy and performance.

Be resilient and persevering Network marketing can be a roller-coaster. Ability to overcome mistakes and maintain an optimistic attitude are crucial. Believe that challenges can be seen as detours, not obstacles. Be committed to your goals, maintain optimism, and be persistent in your actions.

The importance of adopting a "Service" mindset: The most successful network marketers recognize the direct link between their own success as well as others' successes. Choose a more service-oriented mindset and focus on providing the best value to your customers and team members. The goal is to create relationships, build trust and establish a warm community through genuinely caring for their needs, wishes as well as their challenges.

Positive attitude and a positive outlook are crucial to having proper thought process. Your mindset has an enormous effect on your interactions to others since it reflects in your feelings, thoughts and actions.

Here are some ways to building and maintaining positive attitudes:

Accept gratitude It is a good idea to express gratitude for all the blessings in your life like the network marketing business you work for. Be grateful for opportunities and relationships that are brought through, celebrate the small successes along the way be sure to focus your attention to the positive aspects of your travels.

Be surrounded by positive Influences: surround your self with positive role examples. Meet team members, mentors as well as others that are positive, inspirational and dedicated to success. Join groups or networks which promote a positive and positive environment.

It is recommended to use affirmations together with visualization in order to reinforce positive objectives and convictions. Visualize a clear picture of the goals you would like to attain, and then reiterate these frequently using the present tense like they've already accomplished. accomplished.By using this method, you will be able to be able to better link your conscious and subconscious goals.

Self-care and stress management The maintenance of your physical, mental and emotional well-being is vital to maintain a positive outlook.

2.2 Goal Setting and Planning

Set goals and creating plans are essential steps to position your self for success in network marketing. It is possible to focus the efforts of your team, keep track of your progress and keep the drive to achievement by setting goals clearly as well as establishing a strategy. In this article we'll explore the importance of setting goals and planning for networking marketing. We'll also provide tips to assist you in establishing goals that are actually attained.

Why Goal Setting Matters:

Set goals and creating plans are essential steps to position your self for success in network marketing. It is possible to focus on your work, monitor the progress you make, and stay the drive to achievement by establishing clear goals and establishing a plan of action. In this section we'll explore the importance of goal setting and planning for network marketing. We'll provide tips to assist you in establishing goals that can be accomplished.

Measurable progress: Setting goals provides you the opportunity to keep track of the progress and development of your business. These goals help you determine whether you're on the correct direction, and in making any needed adjustments.

Responsibility and Accountability The feeling of accountability can be created by making objectives. The setting of objectives lets you create a system for assessing your progress and setting expectations of yourself. It is your motivation to stay in the right direction and finish the task you've set to accomplish is driven by the accountability.

Creating Effective Goals:

Consider the following suggestions while setting the goals of network marketing:

Make it clear: clearly state your goals. It can be difficult to monitor your progress and make a decisive decision in the event that goals are unclear. If you're looking to "increase sales," for example, make reference to a percentage or income amount.

You must ensure that they can be measured You must ensure that your goals can be quantifiable to track your progress and evaluate the performance of your team. Create precise benchmarks, or metrics which show you've achieved your goal. Establish goals such as gaining the number of clients, or rising to a specific level within the timeframe like.

You must strike a balance between reasonable, realistic goals and stretching goals that push you out of your comfortable area. Goals for stretch push you to push over your current limits to attain new heights. While achievable goals are less laborious and require a lot of effort.

Time-bound: Make your goals an end date to create the feeling of urgency as well as responsibility. It is easier to stay on track and organize your work effectively, and monitor the progress you make by establishing dates.

In order to make goals for the long term easier to manage, break them down into shorter-term objectives.

Creating a Strategic Plan:

Develop a plan of action for your work when you've set your objectives. Take note of the following tasks:

Determine Action steps: Break down your goals into manageable tasks or steps. Determine the specific actions you need to take in order in order to achieve your objectives. The creation of leads, prospecting as well as team-building and improvement, and strategies for marketing are just a few of the activities.

Prioritize the actions you take with respect to priority in order of ascending. Prioritize tasks that have the highest impact and are directly advancing your goals. Sort tasks based on their importance, probability to produce results, and align with the overall plan.

Create a schedule: Lay the steps you will take on the calendar or in a schedule. You can set aside specific times or days to complete various jobs. This helps you organize your time and ensures that each project gets sufficient time.

Monitor and adjust: Always examine your progress with regard to your goals and adjust whenever required. Examine the success of your strategies and adjust according to the latest the feedback of your customers, changes in market and the results of your own research. For better performance Be flexible and ready to change.

Be aware the importance of planning and goal-setting as ongoing actions. Create new goals as you achieve previous ones, in order to continue the process and to make your progress more rapid. Stay in sync with your expanding expectations and goals by frequently revising and altering your plan.

A clear plan in your mind can assist you in getting through the maze of marketing networks with a sense of purpose and certainty.

2.3 Finding Your Why

Find the "why" is a powerful motivational tool that can keep your focus, determined and dedicated to networking marketing. The "why" encapsulates your core reason for joining the profession of networking marketing and striving for the success you desire. Motivation comes from an intrinsic passion. This is crucial during difficult periods. In this chapter, we will talk about the importance of identifying your motivations for networking marketing, and provide advice on how to go about doing that.

Why Your Why Matters:

Your journey to network marketing will be based upon the basis of your "why". It focuses on your primary values, hopes and desires as well as the financial goals you have set for yourself. What is the reason you should find your motivation is explained below:

Motivates: Your drive stems from knowing your purpose. It is easier to keep your commitment, determination and focused on network marketing, even in facing of setbacks or challenges when you are armed with a solid understanding of the reason you're involved in the field.

What drives persistence: Persistence is the key to longevity in the field of the field of network marketing. It can be a challenge. If you have a "why" is strong, you are motivated to push ahead despite difficulties, setbacks or slower advancement. The motivation comes by understanding the reason you are here.

Your reason for being serves as a reflection of your own thoughts and beliefs. It is easy to feel content and enjoy a an inner sense of meaning in the event that your actions align to your ideals. The connection allows you to build a network marketing enterprise that is relevant and authentic to your needs and reflect your core values.

The Decision-Making Guideline: Knowing a clearly defined reason for your decision will help you make the right choices throughout your journey of network marketing. It helps you analyze potential opportunities, understanding tactics and deciding on a path that is in line with your objectives. Your purpose acts as a compass to keep your course, and helping guide your actions in line with your goals for the future.

Finding Your Why:

Reflection on yourself, self-reflection and an in-depth investigation of your motivations for doing business are essential to uncover your motivation. The below methods to discover the personal motivation behind your network marketing:

Be aware of your passions and interests: Think about the things that inspire and excite your most. What passions and interests do you enjoy? Consider the aspects of marketing through networks that align into these hobbies and passions. Consider how networking marketing can allow you to pursue your dreams and help others take action in the same direction.

Find Your Core Values The most important principles that govern your decisions and actions constitute your primary values. Examine how network marketing is compatible to your core values after you have identified the values. Which network marketing strategies can assist you in living a lifestyle which is consistent with your ideals and help improve people's lives?

www.ingramcontent.com/pod-product-compliance
Lightning Source LLC
Chambersburg PA
CBHW071221210326
41597CB00016B/1897